simply BUSINESS

B1+

EFFECTIVE ENGLISH FOR DOING YOUR JOB

ANGELA LLOYD

Cornelsen

Welcome to Simply Business B1+

Who is the book for?

Simply Business is a learner-based course with a hands-on focus, designed to meet the needs of in-work learners who want to use English effectively. The course features real people and companies and uses authentic materials from their day-to-day work.

Reflecting global trends, the course helps you develop awareness and sensitivity towards different accents, varieties of English and cultural differences in communication style.

Simply Business offers plenty of opportunity to apply what you learn to your own work context. Many personalized exercises encourage you to use and adapt the language learned to perform the tasks you have to do on a daily basis. In addition to the functional language, talking points and group projects give you the chance to develop fluency by discussing and presenting workplace-related issues.

How is the book structured?

Simply Business consists of eight units which focus on everyday business communication, working internationally, global English and cultural issues, featuring information and recordings with business people from around the world.

Each unit contains:

- an introduction to the unit topic to get you talking
- topic-related language work using authentic examples of emails, telephone calls, and workplace interaction provided by real business people
- a **Language focus** (1) in which useful grammar or language structures can be practised in context
- **info boxes** (2) and **company boxes** (3) which focus on the situation in your company
- **files** with additional background information and partner exercises
- a **Global English** page, featuring a range of English speakers and focusing on areas that can cause communication breakdown
- an **Over to you** page (4) including a **project** (5) where you can apply what you have learned
- a **Progress check** page with an outlook on the next unit and
- a **footer** (6) which identifies the topic of a page for easy orientation.

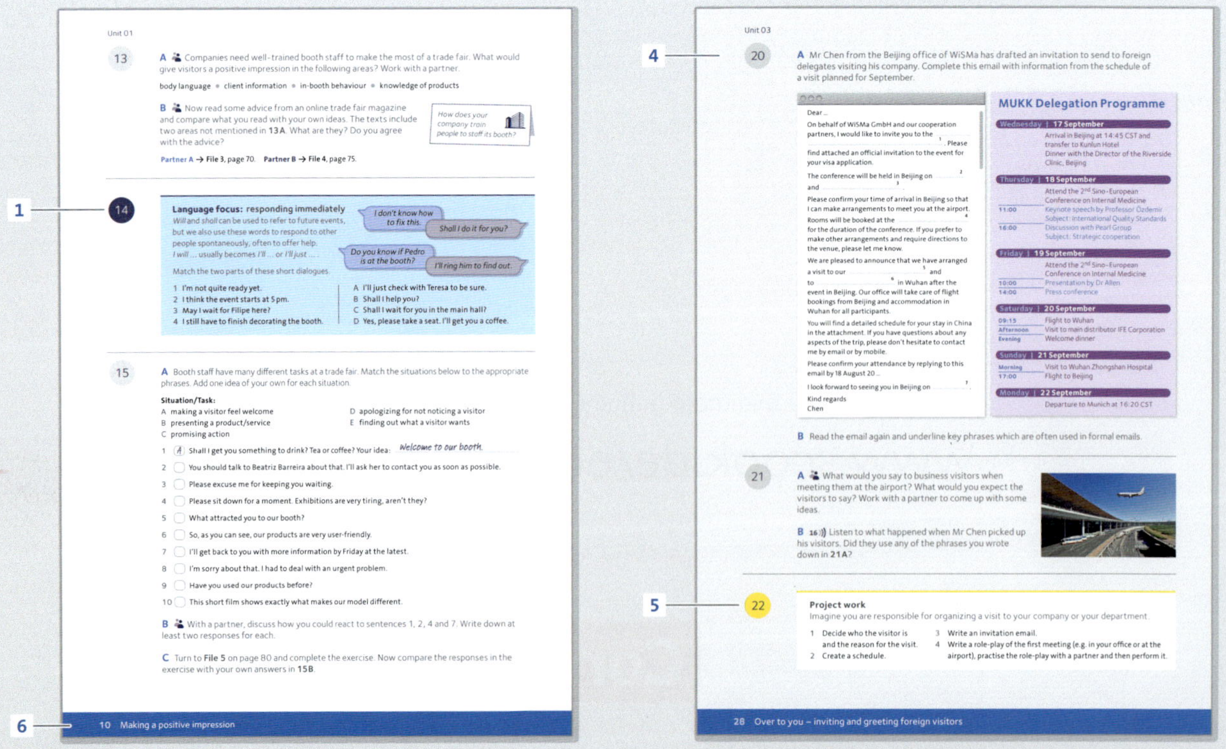

What additional features does Simply Business offer?

- The course includes **four unscripted films with exercises**. The films can be watched during or outside class, but are all directly connected to the unit content. In all the films you see other non-native speakers performing the kind of tasks you may have to do at work. These speakers' English may not always be perfect, but they still communicate their messages effectively to an international audience.

- You have the option of listening to the audios and viewing the films directly on your smartphone or tablet using the **PagePlayer app**. To download the **PagePlayer app** just scan the QR code or go directly to the App Store or Google Play.

When you see an audio))) or a film icon in the book, scan the page using the app and you will be able to listen to or watch the appropriate file.

- A **Vocabulary app** is available from Cornelsen for use with the course. The app uses a flashcard system to practise words and phrases from the book. Once you have installed the free *Cornelsen Vokabeltrainer* app, you may purchase the vocabulary packages which correspond to the B1 or B1+ levels. www.cornelsen.de/vokabeltrainer

- **Word lists**, **Grammar support** and **additional language practice** available online: www.cornelsen.de/simply

We hope you enjoy learning English with Simply Business!

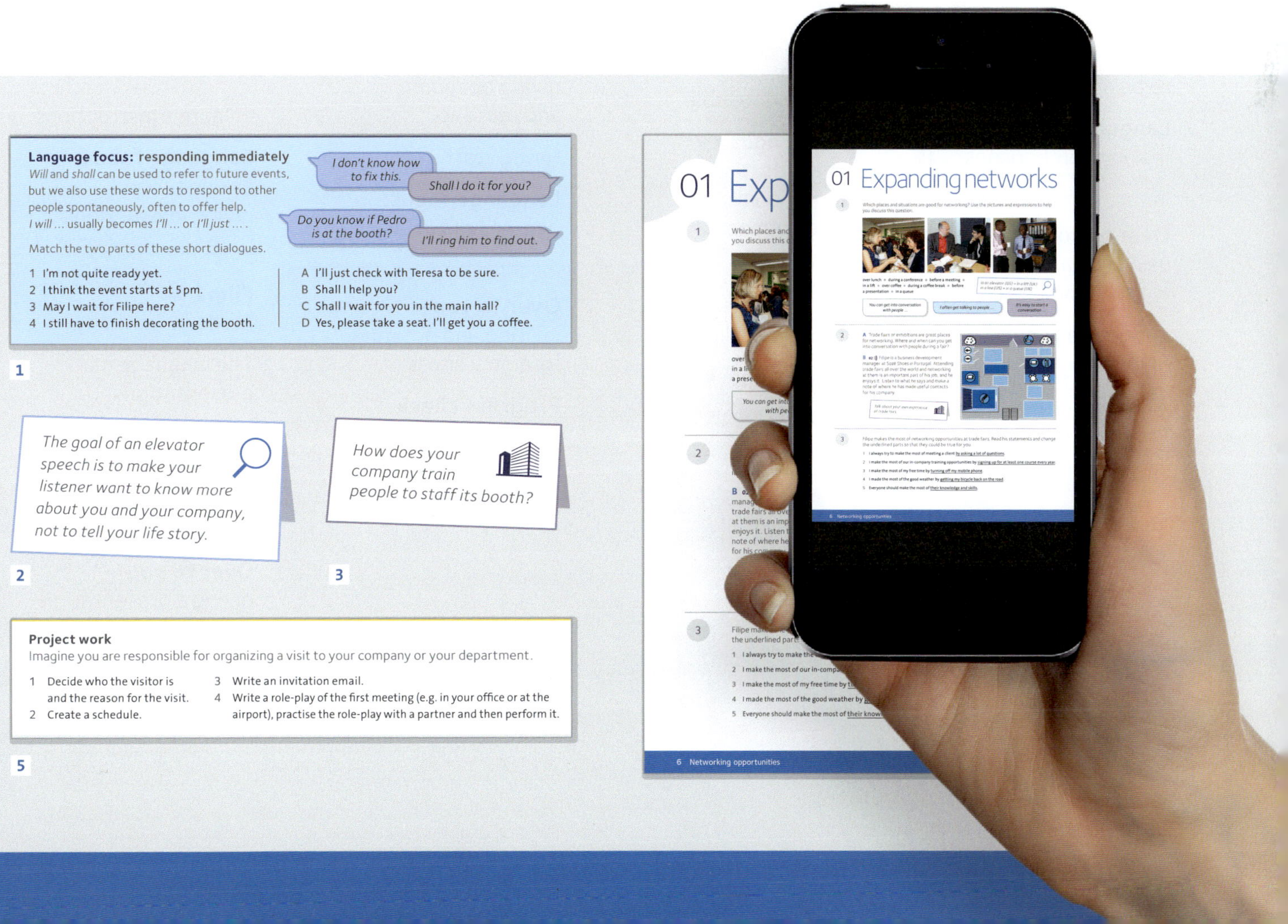

01

02

03

04

01 Expanding networks

1 Which places and situations are good for networking? Use the pictures and expressions to help you discuss this question.

over lunch • during a conference • before a meeting • in a lift • over coffee • during a coffee break • before a presentation • in a queue

in an elevator (US) = in a lift (UK)
in a line (US) = in a queue (UK)

You can get into conversation with people …

I often get talking to people …

It's easy to start a conversation …

---

2 **A** Trade fairs or exhibitions are great places for networking. Where and when can you get into conversation with people during a fair?

B 02 Filipe is a business development manager at Sozé Shoes in Portugal. Attending trade fairs all over the world and networking at them is an important part of his job, and he enjoys it. Listen to what he says and make a note of where he has made useful contacts for his company.

Talk about your own experience of trade fairs.

---

3 Filipe makes the most of networking opportunities at trade fairs. Read his statements and change the underlined parts so that they could be true for you.

1 I always try to make the most of meeting a client by <u>asking a lot of questions</u>.
2 I make the most of our in-company training opportunities by <u>signing up for at least one course every year</u>.
3 I make the most of my free time by <u>turning off my mobile phone</u>.
4 I made the most of the good weather by <u>getting my bicycle back on the road</u>.
5 Everyone should make the most of <u>their knowledge and skills</u>.

4

A What are good topics for breaking the ice with someone you've never spoken to before? Choose the most suitable topics for the situations 1–5. Add your own ideas.

the event • the company • the weather • food • your family • your job • the location • your interests • sport

1 at a trade fair
2 before a job interview
3 at a meal with a client
4 at an office party
5 waiting in a queue in the canteen

to break the ice = to start a conversation

B Discuss your choices with a partner.

C Read the following ice-breakers. Where could they be used? What topics are referred to? There are several possible answers.

1 Isn't it nice to get some fresh air?
2 Have you tried this? It's delicious.
3 It's been a long day, but your booth certainly attracted a lot of interest.
4 Are you staying near the exhibition grounds?
5 I'm very impressed with the way everything was organized.
6 I see that you work for BMI.

5

A If you have started speaking to someone and want the conversation to continue, it is important to be interesting. However, it's even more important to be interested – in your partner! Take it in turns to choose one of the ice-breakers from **4C** as a starting point for a conversation. Your partner responds by answering, adding information and asking a question.

At a trade fair

Are you staying near here?

No, unfortunately not. We left it too late to book a hotel in the city. Did you have better luck?

At a project kick-off meeting

I'm very impressed with the way the meeting was organized.

Me too. I think we've really made the most of our time. What impressed you most?

6

A Once the ice is broken, the next step is to introduce yourself. An elevator speech is a short personal introduction of about 30 seconds to someone you haven't met before. Which of these topics would you mention in this very short time?

age • company • experience • family • hometown • position in company • skills

The goal of an elevator speech is to make your listener want to know more about you and your company, not to tell your life story.

B Imagine you're meeting a group of people for the first time. Choose one of the situations below and make up an elevator speech to introduce yourself. How can you make the information about who you are and what you do sound interesting?

at a trade fair networking event
at the beginning of a presentation
at a sales pitch
at a meeting with a new client
at a meeting to get funding for a project
(your own idea)

7

A How important is the exchange of printed business cards in the digital age? Put a cross on the line to show your opinion, and then explain your reasons to a partner.

essential ←——————————————→ **unnecessary**

B Mark the statements which are true for the exchange of business cards in your business environment. Can you add any more?

1 ☐ Only give your card if someone asks for it.
2 ☐ Leave a business card on the table while you are speaking to the person.
3 ☐ Present your card with both hands.
4 ☐ Make a note of any extra information about your partner on the card.
5 ☐ Use an elegant card holder to store your cards.
6 ☐ When you receive a card, study it and make a comment.

C Business card etiquette is not the same all over the world. Read about the etiquette in other countries and note down some keywords. Use the keywords to summarize what you have read to your partner.

Partner A → **File 1**, page 70. **Partner B** → **File 2**, page 75.

Now compare the new information with the statements in **7B**. What differences do you notice?

8

A Andrea and Karen have met more than once before. How do you know?

Hi Andrea! I was hoping to see you here.

Me too. It's been a long time. When did we last meet? Was it two years ago in Madrid?

B What are the situations here? How could you respond using the pattern of answer, add and ask which Andrea uses in **8A**?

1 It's so nice to meet you again after all this time.
2 Wasn't it you who gave that very interesting demonstration in Prague last year?
3 What a nice surprise! I didn't expect you to be here.
4 Hello again. This is the colleague I was telling you about. Can I introduce you?

9

A Ending a conversation successfully is just as important as breaking the ice. Complete these two conversations at a trade fair with the words below. Which conversation is more informal?

appointment • back • business card • case • chance • excuse • give • here's • hesitate • keep • must • pleasure • soon • sorry

1 If you'll excuse [1] me, I have an appointment [2] with one of our clients in five minutes. Do you have a business card [3] with you? Thank you very much. Here's [4] mine. Please don't hesitate [5] to contact me after the fair. It's been a great pleasure [6] talking to you.

2 I'm sorry [7] but I've just seen someone I must [8] speak to before I go back [9] to the booth. I hope we have a chance [10] to talk again before the fair ends, but let me give [11] you my card just in case [12] so that we can keep [13] in touch. Hope to see you again soon [14].

B Now role-play the following sequence of events with a partner. Make up any details you like.

1 you speak to someone for the first time
2 you bump into each other again later
3 you end the conversation and arrange to keep in contact

to bump into someone = to meet someone by chance

10

A How do you greet the people you come into contact with at work? Read the following greetings and decide whether they are suitable for your work environment.

	always	*it depends*	*never*
Hi Frank	☐	☒	☐
Hello Mrs Ridolfi	☒	☐	☐
Morning Dr Preier	☒	☐	☐
Good morning Engineer García	☐	☐	☒
Sir / Madam	☐	☒	☐

If you marked *it depends*, what does it depend on?

B Now read three comments and decide which one is closest to your way of doing things. Compare your answer with a partner.

"Professional titles are important in a business environment, so we usually address colleagues with Director López or Engineer Beltrán, for example, or perhaps only use the title. With colleagues who we work with on a daily basis, however, we often use first names."

Andrea, Querétaro, Mexico

"I would say that people here always call each other by their first names, whatever their status. The boss will be Elin to everyone, even to the new trainee. If you address someone with a title like "Dr" or "Professor", it almost sounds rude!"

Morten, Trondheim, Norway

"When you meet someone for the first time, it's a good idea to use their title or Mr/Mrs/Ms and the surname. Nonetheless, people usually move on to first names very quickly – sometimes even during the first meeting."

Alessandro, Rome, Italy

11

A Do you sometimes use the English form or the English pronunciation of your name when you introduce yourself in English? If so, why? If not, would you be willing to use a different name with business partners abroad?

B If you do business with Chinese partners or work with Chinese colleagues, you may have noticed that they often use English names. Think of as many reasons as you can for this.

C 03 Listen to Kelsi talk about the role of English names in China. Compare what she says with your answers to **11B**. What else does she say about using western names in China?

D Listen again and make a note of the phrases Kelsi uses to show that what she is saying may not always be true.

When we talk about experiences in another culture, we can only generalize to a certain extent. Different people may have different experiences.

George = Jiří (Czech)
Elizabeth = Alžběta (Czech)
John = Juan (Spanish)
Claire = Chiara (Italian)
Peter = Piotr (Polish)
Eva = Aoife (Irish)

12

Talk about how names and titles are used in your company. What advice would you give a foreigner coming to your country to work or do business? What have you experienced in other companies or countries?

13

A Companies need well-trained booth staff to make the most of a trade fair. What would give visitors a positive impression in the following areas? Work with a partner.

body language • client information • in-booth behaviour • knowledge of products

B Now read some advice from an online trade fair magazine and compare what you read with your own ideas. The texts include two areas not mentioned in **13A**. What are they? Do you agree with the advice?

How does your company train people to staff its booth?

Partner A → **File 3**, page 70. **Partner B** → **File 4**, page 75.

14

Language focus: responding immediately

Will and *shall* can be used to refer to future events, but we also use these words to respond to other people spontaneously, often to offer help. *I will ...* usually becomes *I'll ...* or *I'll just ...* .

I don't know how to fix this.
Shall I do it for you?

Do you know if Pedro is at the booth?
I'll ring him to find out.

Match the two parts of these short dialogues.

1 I'm not quite ready yet.
2 I think the event starts at 5 pm.
3 May I wait for Filipe here?
4 I still have to finish decorating the booth.

A I'll just check with Teresa to be sure.
B Shall I help you?
C Shall I wait for you in the main hall?
D Yes, please take a seat. I'll get you a coffee.

15

A Booth staff have many different tasks at a trade fair. Match the situations below to the appropriate phrases. Add one idea of your own for each situation.

Situation/Task:

A making a visitor feel welcome
B presenting a product/service
C promising action
D apologizing for not noticing a visitor
E finding out what a visitor wants

1 (A) Shall I get you something to drink? Tea or coffee? Your idea: Welcome to our booth.
2 (C) You should talk to Beatriz Barreira about that. I'll ask her to contact you as soon as possible.
3 (D) Please excuse me for keeping you waiting.
4 (A) Please sit down for a moment. Exhibitions are very tiring, aren't they?
5 (E) What attracted you to our booth?
6 (B) So, as you can see, our products are very user-friendly.
7 (C) I'll get back to you with more information by Friday at the latest.
8 (D) I'm sorry about that. I had to deal with an urgent problem.
9 (E) Have you used our products before?
10 (B) This short film shows exactly what makes our model different.

B With a partner, discuss how you could react to sentences 1, 2, 4 and 7. Write down at least two responses for each.

C Turn to **File 5** on page 80 and complete the exercise. Now compare the responses in the exercise with your own answers in **15B**.

16

A People take a variety of factors into account when they are interested in purchasing a product or service. Think about your shoe-buying habits and answer the questions in relation to the factors below.

brand • comfort • company ethics • country of origin • durability • image • material • price • quality • style

1 How often do you buy shoes?
2 Why do you buy new shoes?
3 Where do you buy shoes?
4 When you buy a new pair of shoes, what is important to you?

What I look for is …

What I'm least interested in …

B Which factors do you think are most important for business customers?

17

Language focus: making comparisons

Complete the sentences with the most suitable word.

good – better – best	little – less – least	many/much – more – most
bad – worse – worst	few – fewer – fewest	

1 What our clients are __most__ interested in is how we can help them to be successful.
2 Our US customers are very price-conscious, so they choose the __least__ expensive products.
3 My __worst__ experience was at a trade fair in Las Vegas when our boxes got stuck at customs.
4 Our Asian customers are __more__ likely to attend the fair in Singapore than in Buenos Aires.
5 Unfortunately, we had __fewer__ visitors to the booth this year than last year.

18

A 04 Listen to Filipe and Aoife at the Sozé booth at a trade show in Milan and answer the following questions.

1 Filipe mentions the materials, workmanship, design and price of Sozé shoes. He also talks about social responsibility. What does he say about each of these factors?
2 What action will Filipe and Aoife take after the show?

B Listen again and complete these sentences.

1 What does Filipe say to attract the visitor's attention?

May I ______

2 What does Aoife say to explain why she's interested in the products?

Actually, you know ______

My job now ______

C What criteria are important to you when buying goods or services? Do Filipe's products match your criteria? Look at your answers to **16 A** to help you decide.

19

Imagine you and your partner are staffing your company's booth at a trade fair. What would you say to …

1 ... attract the attention of a visitor?
2 ... describe your company's products/services?
3 ... follow-up after the fair?

If you don't have specific information about your company's products/services, make up any details you like.

20

Language focus: giving advice very directly

Although it is a good idea to choose your words carefully and be diplomatic when giving advice, there are situations where it is more efficient to be direct. For example, when writing a list of dos and don'ts or when we want to tell someone what to do very quickly, it is best to be very clear.

Post information ... | *Remember to ...* | *Don't forget to ...*

05 Listen to a social media consultant talking about how to make the most of a trade show. Finish the sentences based on what he says. Do you agree with his advice?

1 Use your ______
2 Post information ______
3 Introduce ______
4 Run a ______
5 Tweet a ______
6 Take ______

21

A Make verb and noun collocations using the words below.

meet • attend • invite • make • post • run • take

a competition • guests • people • an impression • photos • a show • updates

Collocations are two or more words which are frequently used together.

B Choose two collocations you formed in **21A** and make true sentences about yourself.

Example: meet people *I met a lot of new people at the trade fair last year.*

22

Would these messages persuade you to visit the booths? Why? Why not?

Don't miss today's live demo of Digilit's latest edusoftware.11 am at booth 26, aisle 7, hall 2 **#educomm #lovediglit**

Free at 6 pm? Join PackEx for happy hour at booth 12, aisle 3, main hall. Wine, finger food and a tombola with great prizes! **#interpack16 #packex**

Join #electromobile for free evening tour of downtown Singapore. Meeting point: poster area/hall 1 When? 7 pm/4.10. **www.electromobile.com.cn** **#carsalonsing**

23

Project work

Work with a partner. You are both responsible for your company's social media marketing during a trade fair. You can either choose your own company or make one up.

1 Decide how to use social media to attract attendees to your booth. Look at **File 6** on page 80 for some hints, but decide yourself what you think is helpful.
2 Choose which social media services you want to use and decide what kind of posts will have the greatest impact. Be as inventive as you can!
3 Present your ideas (at least three) to the class.

24 Vocabulary: fixed expressions

There are many fixed phrases which include the words *best*, *worst*, *most* and *least*. Match these phrases with their meanings. Then make up one sentence for each phrase.

1 last but not least	A do as well as possible in a bad situation
2 make the most of	B the most serious thing that can happen
3 make the best of	C get the greatest advantage from
4 the worst case scenario	D a method which shows good results
5 best practice	E last in a list, but not in importance

Now, last but not least, I'd like to demonstrate our new, state-of-the-art coffee machine.

25 Grammar: imperatives

A We can use the same grammatical form for different purposes. Match the sentences and purposes. Make up one additional sentence for each category.

a advice • **b** directions • **c** instructions • **d** invitation • **e** order

1 ☐ Take that chewing gum out of your mouth.
2 ☐ Walk through hall six and turn left at the registration desk.
3 ☐ Come and join us for a glass of wine.
4 ☐ Make sure the appliance is disconnected, then open the back with a screwdriver.
5 ☐ Always send a follow-up email after the show.

B 06 The tone of voice we use depends on the purpose of the sentence we're saying. Listen to the five sentences from **25A** and practise saying each one in the same tone of voice. Then say the sentences you made up using the appropriate tone.

C If the tone is not right, the imperative form can sound rude. Here are some ways to soften what you say by adding a phrase. Soften the imperative sentences in **25A** by adding the following phrases. Sometimes more than one answer is possible.

1 Why don't you ...? 2 First of all, ... 3 It's a good idea to ... 4 Please ... 5 You can ...

26 Useful language

A Complete the following phrases with something you would say during a conversation.

1 It's nice to ...
2 May I ...?
3 Shall we ...?
4 Excuse me, do you ...?
5 I'm very interested in ...
6 If you'll excuse ...
7 Please don't ...
8 I'm sorry, but ...
9 OK, thanks. I ...
10 When I get back, I'll ...

B With a partner, write a dialogue using as many of the sentences you formed in **26A** as you can. Make up any details as you go along.

Before the next class Find out who your company's suppliers and customers are. Prepare to talk about what you know or have found out.

For the next unit Write notes in English on three telephone calls you make this week. How did you introduce yourself and explain why you were calling each time? Did you use any language you would only use on the telephone?

02 Doing a good job

1

A Every company is a link in the chain between a supplier and an end-user. In which position in this chain do you see your own company?

supplier

manufacturer/producer

distributor

end-user

retailer

B At which points in the supply chain would you expect to see the following?

assembly line • components • factory • finished goods • forklift truck • lab • pallets • raw materials • shelves • stock • trucks • warehouse

stock = inventory
truck = lorry

C **07** At What is the difference between a *customer*, a *client* and a *consumer*? Complete the definitions below, then listen and compare. Do you agree with the definitions you hear?

A customer is someone who …
We use the term client for someone who …
When we talk about consumers, we mean …

2

A Read what two people say about their company's activities. What kind of company do you think each one works for? Choose from the options below.

engineering company • fashion retailer • health care provider • IT consultancy • pharmaceutical manufacturer • real estate agency

Our clients are global corporations based in Germany, Switzerland and Austria. We design and implement solutions for today and the future. Our consultants know the relevant software on the market and base their advice on what is best for the client. We work with all the major suppliers, but we do not have agreements with specific suppliers to promote certain products. Our goal is to satisfy each client's unique requirements.

Our customers are manufacturers of cars and commercial vehicles like trucks or buses. We are based in Pune, India, but most of our business is done outside India. We manufacture high-quality products, so we can achieve better price levels in countries like the USA, Germany and Russia, for example. We have a lot of face-to-face meetings with our customers because there are many technical issues to be discussed.

B Use some of the expressions from **2A** to help you describe who your company works with and where your suppliers and clients or customers are based.

3

Language focus: describing processes

1 Every time you order a product online, your purchasing decision is the start of a process. Match the pictures to the descriptions.

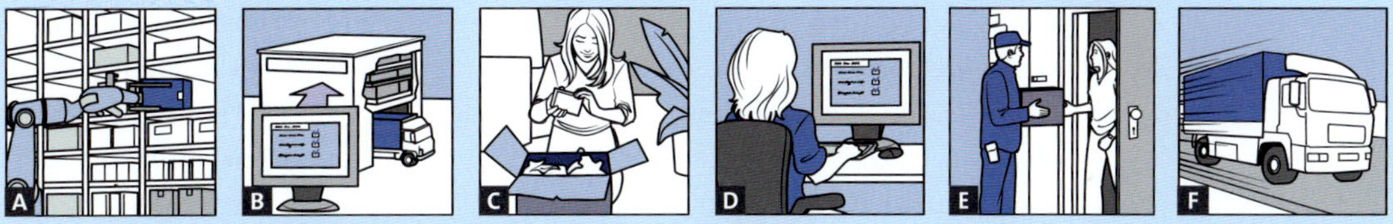

1 (D) The customer places an online order for three products.
2 (B) The order is transmitted to the company warehouse.
3 (A) Products which have been ordered are picked from the warehouse shelves by staff or robots.
4 (C) After an individual order has been assembled, staff pack the items into a shipping box.
5 (F) The box is sent to the shipping bay where trucks are waiting to be loaded.
6 (E) The order is delivered, and the customer unpacks the box.

2 When we describe a process, we usually use a mixture of active and passive sentences. Read the descriptions 1 – 6 again. Underline the active verbs and highlight the passive verbs as in the examples.

A sentence usually starts with the main topic. Within a text, the main topic of a sentence usually reflects back to the sentence before. Any new information comes afterwards.

e.g. The consumer places an online order for three products. The order is transmitted to the company warehouse.

4

A Read the following sentence pairs about the supply chain at a Belgian brewery. One sentence in each pair is active and the other is passive. What impact does this have on the focus of each sentence? Which follow-up sentence is the better choice in each case?

1 Our raw materials are hops, malt, sugar and spices.
 a They are imported from the best European growing regions.
 b We import them from the best European growing regions.

2 This is a small brewery with a limited production capacity.
 a Only one million litres of beer a year is produced here.
 b We only produce one million litres of beer a year here.

3 Some of our beer is bottled here in the brewery and some in other breweries.
 a Bottle lines at big breweries are rented by us to ensure high quality standards.
 b We rent some bottle lines at big breweries to ensure high quality standards.

4 Our customers in Belgium are pubs and retailers.
 a Our beer is also exported to many countries worldwide.
 b We also export our beer to many countries worldwide.

B Create a text about the Belgian brewery's supply chain by combining the sentences in **4A**. Use passive or active sentences according to which one is the best choice for that part of the supply chain. If you need help, look back at the information in the Language focus. Compare your finished text with a partner.

Our raw materials are hops, malt, sugar and spices.

C With a partner, create a flow chart of the supply chain in your company or department. Write captions for each step. Use **3** and **4A** to help you.

What information, materials and equipment do you need to do your job?

5

A Telephone calls have three parts: **a** starting the call, **b** the main message and **c** ending the call. Whatever the reason for the call, what we say in parts **a** and **c** is usually very similar. Read the following phrases and decide whether they belong to part **a** or **c**.

1 ◯ Thanks for your help.
2 ◯ Is this a good time to talk?
3 ◯ You're welcome.
4 ◯ I'm sorry, the line's very bad.
5 ◯ Oh hello, I didn't recognize your voice.
6 ◯ Could I speak to Mr Larsson, please?
7 ◯ What can I do for you?
8 ◯ Thanks for calling.
9 ◯ I'll call back later.
10 ◯ It's Jan here.
11 ◯ I'll speak to you again later.
12 ◯ I'm returning your call.
13 ◯ Please give my regards to Irina.
14 ◯ May I ask who's calling?

B Now decide who could have said each phrase in **5A**. Was it the person making the call, the person receiving the call or either?

caller 2, ______ recipient ______ either ______

C Work with a partner and make a list of more suggestions for what people could say at the beginning and end of a phone call. Mix them up and give them to another pair in your class to sort out.

6

Language focus: on the phone

Most of the language we use on the telephone can also be used in other situations. However, there are some expressions which are only used in telephone calls. Read this list of phrases and decide which ones are **a** only used on the phone, **b** never used on the phone or **c** used on and off the phone.

1 ◯ I'd like to speak to Nico, please.
2 ◯ Hold on, please. I'll put you through.
3 ◯ Is this a good time to talk?
4 ◯ Oh hello, I didn't recognize your voice.
5 ◯ It's been very nice talking to you.
6 ◯ This is Miroslav from head office.
7 ◯ Shall I ask him to call you back?
8 ◯ It's Maria here.
9 ◯ Well, I'd better be going now.
10 ◯ I'm sorry, but Pedro isn't in the office today.
11 ◯ This is Maria again. We were cut off.
12 ◯ May I leave a message for Signora Colozzi?
13 ◯ Who shall I say is calling?
14 ◯ Manuela, I've got Dirk on the line for you.

*It is more common in English-speaking countries than anywhere else to say **How can I help you?** when answering the phone.*

7

Refer to the notes you made on your own phone calls (For the next unit, page 13). Did you write down any phrases that aren't mentioned on this page? Compare what you would say in your own language with the English phrases.

8

A Gertrude Biedermann is a buyer at Sonnentor, an Austrian company which specializes in the production and sale of organic herb mixes and teas. Read what she says about her job and who she deals with. Then complete the following sentence in as many ways as possible.

> *My job involves* collaborating with my colleagues to decide on our purchasing strategy. Together with the other team members, *I'm responsible for* developing our supplier base in line with our customers' needs and our company philosophy. We buy directly from growers of organic products, so *I'm in regular contact with* them in order to be up to date on product availability, to discuss quality standards and to negotiate prices. At Sonnentor, we value close and long-term relationships with our suppliers, so *a lot of my time is spent* making telephone calls and arranging appointments to meet the organic farmers we work with. *It's my job to* stay in close contact with our sales and marketing department because it's vital that I'm aware of customer needs and new trends. *It's always exciting when* new suppliers join our 'family' because this maximizes our ability to offer our customers top quality, innovative products.

Gertrude's job involves ...

B Which suppliers and customers do you deal with in your job? Do you work closely with colleagues from other departments? Write a short profile of your own job using the expressions in *italics* from **8A**.

9

A **08** Cleopa Ayo is planning to visit BioFach in Nuremberg, Germany, one of the leading international trade fairs for organic food. Before the fair, he makes a telephone call to the Sonnentor head office in Austria. Listen and answer the questions.

1 Has he been in contact with Gertrude before?
2 Why does he make the call?
3 What does Gertrude suggest?
4 What do they arrange?

B Read the transcript on page 88 while listening to the phone call again. Underline the parts which give you the answers to the questions in **9A**.

C Listen again and write down the expressions you hear.

1 **Mr Ayo introduces himself:** "__________ Cleopa Ayo from Tanzania. I'm the __________ of Muheza."

2 **Gertrude welcomes Mr Ayo:** "This is Gertrude Biedermann. It's __________."

3 **Cleopa requests a meeting:** "Would that __________?"

4 **Gertrude suggests a day:** "Let me just check my schedule. __________ late Tuesday afternoon?"

5 **Cleopa says which day he prefers:** "Tuesday __________."

6 **Gertrude suggests a suitable time:** "__________ come at 4 pm?"

10

A Think of different ways of suggesting a date for an appointment.

1 What ...? 2 Shall ...? 3 Would ...? 4 Does ...? 5 Are ...?

B Role-play making an appointment with your partner.

11

A What does your supplier or service provider offer? What do customers really want? Sometimes the best way to find out is to simply ask. Choose one of the four situations below and make a list of questions you, as the customer, would ask and would expect to be asked.

at the hairdresser's • at a car dealership • at an electronic goods retailer • at a bank

B Complete these requests from people working in different companies. Which requests are aimed at customers and which at suppliers?

Are you • I would be grateful • How can I • Please tell me • What are • What is your • When can • When will

"__________ 1 reach you outside working hours?"
Anh Tuan, IT Technical Support Agent

"__________ 2 looking for a property to buy or to lease? __________ 3 your requirements regarding location and customer volume?"
Simon, Real Estate Agent

"__________ 4 we expect delivery of the CAD machine?"
Oliver, CEO of an engineering company

"__________ 5 for an update on the availability of the payment cards for our e-wallets."
Mireia, Telecommunications Engineer

"__________ 6 schedule for the day? __________ 7 the last session finish?"
Lily, Corporate Catering

"__________ 8 exactly what the problem is."
Camila, Customer Service Executive

12

A 09 Gertrude and Cleopa are meeting at the trade fair. Listen to what Cleopa is telling Gertrude. What do you think she asked him?

B 10 Now listen to how their conversation goes on. How does Gertrude show her interest in what Cleopa is telling her?

C Gertrude and Cleopa are making arrangements for a Sonnentor representative to visit Tanzania. It is not their first conversation, so they are speaking informally. What phrases do they use in **12B** that mean the same as the following?

1 Would that suit him?
2 I'm afraid, he's not available.
3 That's an excellent idea.
4 Shall we say …?
5 I'm sure that will be convenient for him.

Film 1 If you would like to find out more about Sonnentor's suppliers and customers, watch the film *From field to table*.

Before you watch, turn to the exercises on page 103.

13

A Do you usually start a business telephone call with informal conversation? Read a few opinions from people around the world. Whose answer is closest to yours?

I work in a technical department and we get straight to the point. People in Marketing are different! Some small talk is necessary if you are speaking to someone of higher status or to someone you've never met. I would always start by asking if the person is busy and finish by apologizing for bothering the person. *Lisha, Nanjing, China*

Informal talk is common on the phone when people of the same status know each other personally. Women probably spend more time on this than men. Apart from in small family companies, bosses are taken very seriously, so would not tolerate any chit-chat during a business call. *Janet, Nairobi, Kenya*

All phone calls start with some informal conversation. This doesn't depend on the status or gender of the speakers. *Elano, Florianopolis, Brazil*

We like to do business on a personal and friendly basis, so when speaking to clients, it's polite to start with some general conversation like 'I guess it must be hot in Chennai right now.' or 'Have you been very busy at work?' Of course, it also depends on status. If I had a meeting with my boss, I would stick to the agenda unless he initiated a personal conversation. *Manjul, New Delhi, India*

We prefer to get straight to the point of the phone call. To us, it seems rude to waste the other person's time with what we think of as unnecessary small talk. *Ole, Bergen, Norway*

B How would you respond if someone said these things to you during a business telephone call?

1 Are you busy?
2 How was your holiday?
3 Sorry to have bothered you.
4 It's Pete here. What about the meeting next week?
5 Please give my regards to Thomas.
6 It was so nice meeting you at the trade fair last month.

14

A What are the challenges and advantages of using the phone to communicate internationally? Think about these topics.

a accents • **b** efficiency • **c** misunderstandings • **d** names • **e** purpose • **f** relationship building • **g** speaking styles • **h** telephone connection • **i** time

What is your own experience of making international phone calls?

B Why would you say this? Match each sentence with a topic or topics from **14 A.** In some cases, more than one answer is possible.

1 ☐ The reason I'm calling is ...
2 ☐ Sorry, I didn't catch that.
3 ☐ Do you have a few minutes?
4 ☐ So, do you mean ...?
5 ☐ Can you hear me better now?
6 ☐ Nice to talk to you. How's life in ...?
7 ☐ Could you say that again a bit more slowly, please?
8 ☐ So, we agree that ...

I would say this in order to ...

I would say this if I didn't ...

C Role-play a telephone call with your partner. Don't face each other while you talk and/or use your telephone.

Partner A → **File** 7, page 71. **Partner B** → **File** 8, page 75.

15

A What would be important to you about the quality of goods or services if you were …

1 … a consumer buying **a** organic food or **b** a property (a house or flat)?
2 … a business customer **a** employing an IT consultancy or **b** buying forklift trucks for the warehouse?

B One aspect of quality is the availability of goods and services. Here are some ways of talking about availability:

☑ It's *in stock.*	☒ It's *out of stock* at the moment.
☑ It's *available for immediate delivery.*	☒ It *won't be available* for at least six weeks.
☑ We *can provide* this service.	☒ It's *no longer available.*
☑ We *can supply* you.	☒ We are *unable to provide* this service.
	☒ We are *no longer able to provide* this service.

Now choose the most suitable phrases and complete the following sentences.

1 We are having some problems with our supplier, so the parts you ordered are ______________ stock at the moment. They ______________ until early next year.
2 I have some good news. The black pepper from Tanzania is ______________ delivery.
3 We are ______________ service at the moment because of technical problems at head office.

16

A Read the text on Quality Management in companies and decide which underlined words or phrases have the same meaning as the words below.

1 be fit for purpose	3 comply with	5 guarantee	7 meet
2 certified	4 enable	6 label	8 requirements

For consumers, quality means products are long-lasting and reliable. The concept of quality for companies is more complicated. Products and services must satisfy customer expectations and do what they are intended to do.
Quality Management Systems are implemented to allow companies to compare the quality of their products and processes with industry standards. These measures ensure that customers get good quality. In many industries, it is necessary to be accredited according to international standards like ISO 9001.
Based on the ISO 9001 process management model, there are other accreditation programmes which give a quality seal to companies in a particular industry which conform to the highest standards.

B A Quality Management System (QMS) improves the processes in a company and implements measures to increase the value of the business. What measures could be implemented by **a** an organic food retailer, **b** a real estate agency, **c** an IT consultancy and **d** a manufacturer of forklift trucks to guarantee that customers are satisfied?

We ensure high quality by …

Our products are tested …

Our staff/products/services/ processes are … by …

17

Project work

Talk about the quality aspects of your company's products or services.

1 Describe how you, your department or your company provide quality to your customers or clients.
2 Which is the most effective medium (e.g. email, presentation, short video) for communicating the quality aspects of your company's products or services to a customer, to your boss or to another department in your company? Why?

18 Grammar: passive

Complete this description of a company's activities by choosing the active or passive form of the verbs in brackets.

1 WiSMa ________________ (provide) services in the medical sector and ________________ (trade) in medical equipment.

2 The equipment ________________ (supply) to us by German and British manufacturers.

3 We ________________ (authorize) by them to be their exclusive agents in China.

4 Our Beijing office ________________ (organize) medical conferences in the field of dental medicine.

5 The next conference ________________ (plan) for next September.

6 We ________________ (hope) to expand our activities to other aspects of health care.

19 Listening: telephoning language

A Complete these telephoning phrases.

1 The ________ is very bad. I can hardly hear you.

2 Can I call you ________ later?

3 Please wait a moment. I'll try to ________ you ________ .

4 Would you like to leave a ________ ?

5 ________ for calling.

B 11 Listen to six excerpts from telephone conversations and identify what each caller wants. Listen again and make a note of how you would respond to each one.

C 12 Now listen to the responses and compare them to the responses you came up with in **19B**.

20 Useful language

Form suitable questions for the answers 1–6 using *How* and the words below. Pay attention to the underlined parts of the sentences.

big • far • long • many • much • soon

1 How ________________________ ?
– We can deliver the first batch by September 1st.

2 How ________________________ ?
– The nearest port is Mombasa. It's about 200 miles away.

3 How ________________________ ?
– We produce 1 million litres per year.

4 How ________________________ ?
– We have a workforce of 310 at this location.

5 How ________________________ ?
– The total transit time from Shanghai to Rome is 26 days.

6 How ________________________ ?
– We stock 700 different products.

Before the next class Find out which countries your company does business with. Choose one country and prepare to talk about the business relationship.

For the next unit Do you ask or tell people to do things in the course of your job? Make a note of some of the things you say on a regular basis.

03 Going global

1

A Use the photos and the verbs below to talk about the different ways companies operate internationally.

assemble • export • import • manufacture • outsource • purchase • recruit • research • sell • source • take over • trade

One way is to outsource …

Some companies operate internationally by …~ing …

Our company was taken over by …

B What products or services could these comments refer to? Rewrite them by replacing the underlined parts with the names of specific products and services. Then compare your ideas with a partner and explain your choices.

1 "The components for our products are manufactured in China."
2 "We import raw materials from Russia."
3 "Certain services have been outsourced to India."
4 "The USA is an important market for our products."
5 "The raw materials we need for our products are sourced and purchased in Italy."
6 "Our products/services are sold all over the world."

2

A Choose the correct verb forms to complete this definition of acronyms which are often used when discussing world trade.

Acronyms such as BRICS, MINT, CIVETS and CAPPT (refer / are referred)[1] to groups of countries which (consider / are considered)[2] to be at a similar stage of development. They (represent / are represented)[3] a shift of economic power from the G7 countries to the developing world. The terms (use / are used)[4] very widely by business analysts.

An acronym is an abbreviation which is said as a word, e.g. OPEC.

B BRICS, MINT, CIVETS and CAPPT: Do you know which country each letter refers to? Work with a partner to find out.

Partner A → **File 9**, page 71. **Partner B** → **File 10**, page 76.

C Turn back to what you found out about your company's global operations (Before the next class, page 21) and discuss these questions in class.

1 Which of the countries mentioned in **2B** does your company do business with? What kind of business relationships do you have with them?
2 If your company doesn't have business contacts with any of these countries yet, which might be a good source of suppliers, customers or business partners?

3

Are any abbreviations or acronyms widely used in your company or in your department? Do any of them refer to English terms? Write down a few, then find out if your partner knows what the letters stand for. Use the expressions you learned in **2B** to ask and answer each other's questions.

4

A There are many abbreviations which are used to refer to time. How do we say the ones below? What do they mean? Do you know any more?

am • pm • GMT • BRT • CET • CST • 24/7

In many countries, people would be surprised to hear someone say "Let's meet at thirteen thirty."

B Countries have different systems for writing the date. Can you guess which format the following countries use for 18 August 2016? One country uses all three formats.

A 18/08/16	B 16/08/18	C 08/18/16
1 ☐ Brazil	4 ☐ India	7 ☐ Turkey
2 ☐ Canada	5 ☐ Italy	8 ☐ UK
3 ☐ China	6 ☐ Japan	9 ☐ US

Which system is used in your country? Which seems most logical to you? What do you think is the best way to write dates when you are working internationally?

5

A What impact could the following time factors have on companies which operate globally?

holiday periods • summer time / winter time • time zones • the working week

It might be difficult to reach … | *You can't be sure that …* | *It depends on …*

B Find out more about the four time factors mentioned in **5A**. Make a note of keywords while you are reading. Use your notes to tell your partner what you have read.

Partner A → **File 11**, page 71. **Partner B** → **File 12**, page 76.

C 13 Which issues from **5B** do you think are most difficult to deal with? Listen and make notes on what Amar and Daniela say. Do you have the same experience?

6

A Appointments, meetings, schedules and deadlines are part of everyone's working life. Which of the verbs below can be used to talk about **a** an appointment, **b** a deadline, **c** a meeting and **d** a schedule? You can use the verbs more than once.

agree on • arrange • delay • extend • meet • miss • plan • postpone • prepare • set

B Match the expressions which have the same or similar meanings. More than one combination may be possible. Can you add any more?

1 ahead of schedule	A a break
2 behind schedule	B early
3 on schedule	C immediately
4 right away	D in a hurry
5 time off	E late
6 time out	F on time
7 under time pressure	
8 without delay	

Are you on schedule with your project?

No, we missed the deadline again!

C Use a few expressions from **6A** and **6B** to ask your partner about his/her work schedule and projects.

7

A Underline the phrases in these sentences which we use to ask people to do things. Discuss how friendly/unfriendly or direct/indirect each one sounds.

a Do you think you could send me the report by tomorrow morning, please?
b I'm sure we'll need to explain this in more detail to the client next week.
c Could I ask you to contact me again later today?
d You'll need to check those figures again, I'm afraid.
e I need you to ask someone from head office to deal with this.
f I'd like to see some results before the end of the week.

we'll = we will
you'll = you will
I'd = I would

B Choose the most suitable response to each request in **7A**. How else could you respond to each one?

1 ▢ I think you're right. Would you like me to prepare something for the meeting?
2 ▢ Yes, of course. Who's the best person to ask?
3 ▢ OK. I'll get back to work immediately.
4 ▢ Certainly, I've nearly finished it.
5 ▢ Yes, I know. There's something wrong somewhere.
6 ▢ No problem. I'll get back to you after lunch.

C Think about your own job (For the next unit, page 21). Then choose four of the underlined phrases in **7A** and write down sentences you might say at work. Who would you say them to?

8

Language focus: explaining why something is/was impossible
If we have to give bad news, we often use a phrase to "soften" the message.

Before the bad news:

I'm afraid … | *I'm sorry, but …* | *Unfortunately, …* | *To be honest, …*

After the bad news:

We apologize for this. | *I'm very sorry about this.*

We use expressions with the present or past progressive to explain why we can't or couldn't do something. For example:
I *can't reach* Tanya because *she's spending* her holiday in her summer house.
I *can't meet* the deadline because *I'm waiting for* some figures from Marketing.
Tuesday *isn't convenient* for me because *I'm having* some time off next week.
I *couldn't answer* your call because *I was having* a meeting with a client.
We *had to stop* the project because our client *was having* a lot of financial problems.

Complete these sentences in ways which could be true for you. Then add a suitable softening phrase to each one.

1 I can't … because I'm … ~ing …
2 We can't … because … is/are … ~ing …
3 I couldn't … because the client was … ~ing …
4 My boss couldn't … because … was … ~ing …

9

9 Complete a diary page with typical activities you do at work. Use the ideas you had in **7C** to help you.

Partner A → **File 13**, page 72. **Partner B** → **File 14**, page 77.

10

Discuss these questions from a questionnaire about cultural perspectives.

1 How would you explain the difference in the meaning between the words "cheap" and "inexpensive"? When would you use each one?

2 How many different interpretations can you think of for the phrase "that's interesting"?

3 Does the word "compromise" refer to something positive or negative?

4 People from different countries sometimes see everyday things in different ways. What associations with the words in ***bold*** could other people have?

*For me, **lunch** is only a sandwich.*

*People who can't afford a car ride **bicycles**.*

*A **holiday** is a time to visit family.*

You can check the answers in **File 15** on page 81.

11

How do you use the word *problem*? Read what others from around the world have to say. Which is closest to the way you use the word?

Our word for problem is *masalah*. This is always something very serious.
Nando, Indonesia

We often use the word *Problem*. For example, I would say that I had a problem getting here, even though I'm here so it couldn't have been that difficult! *Maren, Germany*

The smallest thing may be a *problema* – like I don't know what to wear to go out this evening!
Mateo, Italy

It's hard to find an equivalent for the word problem in Chinese. I suppose we would say *wèn tí*. The two words mean question and topic. I suppose we don't like to talk about problems! *Liu, China*

Ladies and gentlemen, this is your captain speaking. We have a small problem. All four engines have stopped. We are doing our damnedest to get them going again. I trust you are not in too much distress.
Flight Captain Eric Moody of British Airways Flight 009 flying from London Heathrow to Auckland, New Zealand on 24 June 1982

*Native speakers of English are most likely to use the words **challenge** and **issue** instead of **problem**.*

12

Read a list of possible ways of refusing a request. What are the pros and cons of each? How do you prefer to say *no*?

1 I'm afraid that's impossible.
2 It might be difficult.
3 We'll do our best.
4 No way!
5 (silence)
6 Yes, OK.
7 I wish I could help you.
8 I'm sorry, but I'll have to say no because ...

13

What impact could the fact that the same words may be used in different ways have on how you work with international partners?

14

A Each partner is going to read about the activities of a company. While reading, note down a few keywords (location, business field, main activities, reasons for going global, etc.).

Partner A → **File 16**, page 72. **Partner B** → **File 17**, page 77.

B Exchange information about the companies with your partner by asking and answering questions. Try to do this using your notes and without referring back to the text.

What kind of company is it?

Did you find out why they've gone global?

They have a subsidiary in …

They offer a range of products and services.

Refer to what you found out in Before the next class, page 21 to describe your company's global operations.

15

Language focus: giving opinions and reasons

1 Which of the expressions in *italics* are giving **a** opinions and **b** reasons?

1 ☐ *It makes sense* to recruit local staff.
2 ☐ *If you ask me*, it's better to outsource certain operations.
3 ☐ *For one thing*, it's cheaper to manufacture in Asia.
4 ☐ *Another reason* for opening a factory there is the excellent infrastructure.
5 ☐ *I say that because* the Chinese market is very important to us.
6 ☐ *I agree with you* that we have to act quickly.

2 Which sentence ending is closest to your opinion? Use the expressions above and any other suitable phrases you know to help you explain why.

1 When a company goes global, …
☐ its revenue increases.
☐ it risks losing money.

2 If your company sends you to work abroad, …
☐ you need to learn the local language.
☐ you don't need to learn the local language.

16

A 14 You are going to find out more about the global operations of Chemi and WiSMa. Listen and make a note of why the company you read about in **14 A** choose to expand to Brazil or China.

factory = production plant

B Now tell your partner about your company's reasons for choosing to expand to each location. How is the focus of each one different?

C Chemi and WiSMa are different in many ways. Discuss the differences you noticed.

Chemi is a manufacturing company, WiSMa, on the other hand, …

It doesn't say so, but I think Chemi has more …

Both companies work in the medical sector, but …

WiSMa provides a variety of services, whereas Chemi …

17

Language focus: degrees of certainty

When we give an answer or an opinion, we may be **more** or **less** certain that we are right.

It must be an advantage to speak the local language.
It must have a positive impact on my career.
There must be a better way of dealing with this issue.

It might/could be better to have a face-to-face meeting.
It might/could result in higher productivity.
There might/could be some advantages if we hire local staff.

Now form your own sentences using the sentence beginnings above.

18

A You have learned about Chemi's operations in Brazil and WiSMa's activities in China. Which option would each company choose in order to ensure good communication between head-quarters and the office or plant abroad? Why do you think so?

1 local workers or expat workers
2 local management or expat management
3 regular visits or conference calls
4 English as the working language or not

Expats or expatriates are people who live and work outside their home country, usually for a limited time and sometimes sent by their employers.

B 15))) Now listen to find out how Chemi and WiSMa handled going international. What did they do and what were their reasons?

19

Would you like to work for your company abroad? Look at the pictures and think about what you would enjoy and what might be difficult for you. Add ideas of your own and prepare to give your opinion and explain your reasons.

20

A Mr Chen from the Beijing office of WiSMa has drafted an invitation to send to foreign delegates visiting his company. Complete this email with information from the schedule of a visit planned for September.

Dear ...

On behalf of WiSMa GmbH and our cooperation partners, I would like to invite you to the ______ 1. Please find attached an official invitation to the event for your visa application.

The conference will be held in Beijing on ______ 2 and ______ 3.

Please confirm your time of arrival in Beijing so that I can make arrangements to meet you at the airport. Rooms will be booked at the ______ 4 for the duration of the conference. If you prefer to make other arrangements and require directions to the venue, please let me know.

We are pleased to announce that we have arranged a visit to our ______ 5 and to ______ 6 in Wuhan after the event in Beijing. Our office will take care of flight bookings from Beijing and accommodation in Wuhan for all participants.

You will find a detailed schedule for your stay in China in the attachment. If you have questions about any aspects of the trip, please don't hesitate to contact me by email or by mobile.

Please confirm your attendance by replying to this email by 18 August 20.. .

I look forward to seeing you in Beijing on ______ 7.

Kind regards
Chen

MUKK Delegation Programme

Wednesday | 17 September

Arrival in Beijing at 14:45 CST and transfer to Kunlun Hotel
Dinner with the Director of the Riverside Clinic, Beijing

Thursday | 18 September

Attend the 2nd Sino-European Conference on Internal Medicine

11:00	Keynote speech by Professor Özdemir Subject: International Quality Standards
16:00	Discussion with Pearl Group Subject: Strategic Cooperation

Friday | 19 September

Attend the 2nd Sino-European Conference on Internal Medicine

10:00	Presentation by Dr Allen
14:00	Press conference

Saturday | 20 September

09:15	Flight to Wuhan
Afternoon	Visit to main distributor IFE Corporation
Evening	Welcome dinner

Sunday | 21 September

Morning	Visit to Wuhan Zhongshan Hospital
17:00	Flight to Beijing

Monday | 22 September

Departure to Munich at 16:20 CST

B Read the email again and underline key phrases which are often used in formal emails.

21

A What would you say to business visitors when meeting them at the airport? What would you expect the visitors to say? Work with a partner to come up with some ideas.

B 16 Listen to what happened when Mr Chen picked up his visitors. Did they use any of the phrases you wrote down in **21A**?

22

Project work

Imagine you are responsible for organizing a visit to your company or your department.

1. Decide who the visitor is and the reason for the visit.
2. Create a schedule.
3. Write an invitation email.
4. Write a role-play of the first meeting (e.g. in your office or at the airport), practise the role-play with a partner and then perform it.

23 Vocabulary: writing emails

A Emails can be formal or informal. Match the formal expressions with their more informal equivalents.

1 On behalf of ..., I would ...
2 Please find attached ...
3 ... will be held at ...
4 Please confirm your ...
5 Hotel reservations have been made at ...
6 If you require directions to the venue, ...
7 We're pleased to announce ...
8 Please don't hesitate to contact me if ...

A Please let us know your ...
B I'm glad to inform you that ...
C Drop me a line if ...
D If you want to know how to get to ...
E I'm sending ...
F I've booked rooms at ...
G We would ...
H ... will take place at ...

B Rewrite Mr Chen's formal email in exercise **20A** in a more informal style.

24 Useful phrases

A 17 Listen to Alex and Maria discussing the progress of a project and find expressions similar to the following.

1 There's not much time.
2 as planned
3 immediately
4 postpone
5 early
6 finish on time

B You heard the expressions *working around the clock* and *to give someone breathing space* in **24A**. What do you think they mean?

C Complete these sentences with a suitable time expression from below. Write your own sentences for the ones you didn't use.

behind schedule • busy schedule • in time • overtime • time off • time-out • time pressure

1 Alex isn't in today, he's having some ______________ .
2 If we work ______________ , we might meet the deadline.
3 The developers were under a lot of ______________ to finish their work.
4 Don't worry we'll be there ______________ for the meeting.

25 Vocabulary: word puzzle

A Work with a partner to complete the word puzzle.

Partner A → **File 18**, page 72. **Partner B** → **File 19**, page 77.

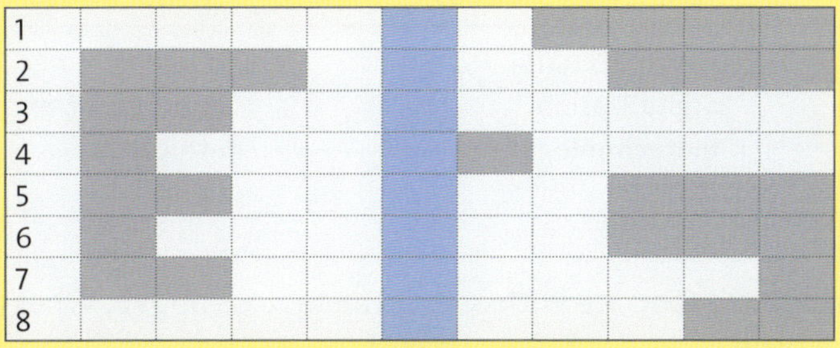

B Write a clue for the word in the blue column.

Before the next class What is special about your company? Note down at least four points and bring them to the next lesson.

For the next unit Make notes on what comes to your mind when you think of business presentations. Prepare to explain your ideas in class.

04 Looking ahead

1

A Products often change their appearance and sometimes even their function over the years. Discuss what has happened to the telephone.

At first … | *The next development was …* | *Later …* | *A new innovation was …* | *The latest trend is …*

B The lifecycles of products vary. Some products stay the same for a long time, others change or even disappear after a short time. What can you say about these two products?

We say that something is ***the greatest thing since sliced bread*** *if it is a really great invention.*

C Brainstorm products or services that **a** are no longer around, **b** have remained largely the same and **c** have gone through various changes since their invention. What do you think were the reasons for this? Discuss with a partner.

… seems so outdated now. | *There's no demand for … because …* | *… was such an innovative idea that …* | *Technology has developed so fast in the field of …, so …*

D Complete these comments with your own opinions.

A walkman was so …
A satnav is such a …
One new product that I find very useful is …
It's such a shame that …

How have the products or services your company provides changed over time?

2

A When companies develop new products, they consider future trends. What products or services do you associate with the following factors? Can you add any more?

Social trends	Technological trends	Environmental trends
customer-specific products	new materials	mobility
demographics	digitalization	energy efficiency
regional development	biotechnology	ethics

B Think of a company which you associate with one of the factors above. What do they do? If you need help, look back at the companies in units 1 – 3.

3

A Read about the activities of three innovative companies. Then complete the sentences to help you exchange information with your partners.

Partner A **Piacentini Costruzione SpA, Modena** *Made in Italy*

As a major Italian construction and civil engineering company, we are one of the global market leaders in steel sheet pile technology. One of our projects is the construction of the harbour in Al-Zawiya, Libya. Using this technology, we can build an entirely new harbour within a short period of time and at a reasonable price while meeting the shipping industry's demands for deeper harbours. An added advantage is that the environmental impact of sheet piles is considerably lower compared to other technologies. For example, the service time under water is longer and the steel piles can be re-used. All this makes our steel sheet pile technology ideal for countries like Libya which have an urgent need to develop their infrastructure.

Partner B **WeDoTech, Porto** *Made in Portugal*

WeDoTech is an R & D company which develops innovative technologies, products and services in the fields of biotechnology and engineering. We provide specialized substances (media) for classic biofilters, using raw materials from Portuguese woodlands. These media can be used in combination with other materials to suit different applications. An added advantage of these media is that they are low-maintenance and easy to handle either manually or mechanically. Our biological treatment technologies are effective options for dealing with air pollution and are environmentally sustainable alternatives to chemical treatment methods.

Partner C **service-drone, Berlin** *Made in Germany*

Civilian-use drones have revolutionized many areas of our lives, and service-drone is a market leader in the development of micro drone flight systems. Our main area of expertise is the production of drones for film production, but our drones are also used for mapping, measuring and industrial documentation. We work closely with our clients in order to manufacture a product according to their unique specifications. The outstanding features of our drones are low noise, long flight time and stable flight position. An added advantage is that they are easy and safe to handle, even for beginners.

1 ... operates in the ... industry.
2 The main area of expertise of ... is ...
3 What is innovative about the company is that ...
4 An added advantage of ... is that ...

B Will there be a market for the products in **3A** in ten years? Why do(n't) you think so? Will it be necessary to modify them in the future?

4

Language focus: making a good impression

1 Circle the word or phrase in each pair which sounds more impressive to you. Which ones were used in the company texts in **3A**?

1	a) new	b) innovative	5	a) unique	b) particular
2	a) change	b) revolutionize	6	a) expertise	b) knowledge
3	a) sustainable	b) long-term	7	a) much	b) considerably
4	a) big	b) major	8	a) great	b) outstanding

2 Write a short description of what your company does using your own information (Before the next class, page 29) and the company texts in **3A**. If necessary, add a picture or diagram. Use the words you chose above to make a very positive impression.

5

A What has happened here?
What did the man really mean?

B Some expressions are difficult to understand even if you know all the words. Read the examples below. Do you understand all the words? What do think the expressions mean?

1 You see?
2 The meal was sort of expensive.
3 See you later.
4 Take it easy.
5 Let's keep in touch.
6 Oh, come on!
7 Never mind.
8 It's up to you.
9 Thank goodness for that.

Check the answers in **File 20** on page 81.

C Choose four expressions from **5B** and say how you would respond. Do you use the same expressions in your own language?

6

The pictures illustrate common sayings in four different languages. They all mean the same thing. What could the meaning be?

Check the answer in **File 21** on page 81. If your language was not one of the four mentioned, what would you say in this context?

7

A *Reading between the lines* is a common saying in many languages. Can you think of any other sayings which are more or less the same in English and in your own language?

B Sometimes it's very difficult to guess the meaning of common sayings because they are based in the culture of the country.

1 Can you guess what the Norwegian saying *hoppe etter Wirkola* (It's like jumping after Wirkola) means?
2 What about this saying from Brazil/Portugal: *só para inglês ver* (He does it so the English can see it)?

18 Now listen to find out if you were right.

C Why do we use so many idiomatic expressions in our native language? What are the problems of using idiomatic expressions in another language? Do you think it is better not to use idioms when communicating internationally in English? Discuss these questions with a partner, then compare your opinions in class.

8

Think of common examples of idiomatic language in your native language. Now be innovative in your use of English by translating the expressions into English and explaining what they mean.

9

A When did you last give or get some advice? Use these sentences to talk about your own experiences at work or at home. Adapt the sentences as you like.

1 I advised ... on how to ...
2 ... suggested that ... would be a good idea.
3 ... asked for my advice on how to ...
4 I pointed out that ... would be ...

to advise (verb)
advice (noun)

B What was your reaction the last time someone gave you advice?

I didn't ask for her advice, so I ...

... had a very good point so, ...

The advice was very helpful, so ...

10

Language focus: advising and convincing

To show that you are giving good advice, do the following: **a** show the benefits of your advice, **b** be open, **c** base your advice on facts, **d** build trust and **e** be optimistic.

1 Match these phrases with the strategy **a** – **e** being used.

1 ☐ My reason for advising you to change to the new technology is ...
2 ☐ I understand the problems that you're having, so I would suggest that we ...
3 ☐ This technology will enable you to reduce costs by ...
4 ☐ I have no doubt that this decision will ...
5 ☐ Surveys show that there is a demand for ...

2 Rephrase the sentences above.

1 If you change to the new technology, *you will see the benefits immediately.*
2 If you want to solve the problems you're having, ...
3 If you want to reduce costs, ...
4 If you take this decision now, ...
5 If you study the survey results, ...

3 We can give more emphasis to what we say by adding words like *completely, definitely, drastically, entirely* and *totally*. Rewrite these sentences with more emphasis. In some cases, there is more than one possible answer.

1 This is a new idea.
2 This will reduce our costs.
3 We're not satisfied with the performance of the new machine.
4 We're interested in hearing more about your proposal.

11

A 19 It is not always easy to introduce changes to a customer or within a company. Listen to two short dialogues and decide whether the customer or colleague is accepting or rejecting the changes being suggested.

B Listen again and write down the phrases which gave you the answers in **11A**.

12

A Work with a partner and choose one of these situations. Look back at page 31 to check information about Piacentini Costruzione or WeDoTech. Make up any extra details.

Role-play 1
A meeting between a representative of the local government of a seaside town and the Italian construction and civil engineering company Piacentini Costruzione.

Partner A → **File 22**, page 72. **Partner B** → **File 24**, page 78.

Role-play 2
A meeting between the CEO of a plant for agricultural waste water treatment and WeDoTech, an R & D company in the field of biotechnology and engineering.

Partner A → **File 23**, page 73. **Partner B** → **File 25**, page 78.

13

A Look at the list and tick the situations you deal with in your job.

1 ▢ Explaining a process
2 ▢ Giving instructions to a client
3 ▢ Asking technical support for help
4 ▢ Demonstrating how something works
5 ▢ Following instructions on how to use equipment

B What differences might there be in the way someone gives instructions? How would you give instructions to a (potential) customer, a trainee, someone who doesn't speak your language very well or someone who is doing something for the first time?

14

Language focus: asking for and giving instructions

1 Complete these requests for help.

about • best • help • how • next • step • through • work

1 What's the first ______ ?
2 Excuse me, can you ______ me with something?
3 Can you show me ______ to do this?
4 How does this ______ ?
5 Can you talk me ______ this?
6 What's the ______ way to do this?
7 What do I do ______ ?
8 How do I go ______ doing that?

2 When giving instructions, we use phrases to **a** signal we're moving on to the next step, **b** explain why we do something, **c** check understanding and **d** accompany a demonstration. What is the purpose of each of the following phrases?

1 ▢ After you've done that, ...
2 ▢ You see?
3 ▢ Look, here, like this.
4 ▢ If you turn this switch, you'll ...
5 ▢ As you can see ...
6 ▢ Finally, ...
7 ▢ Then ...
8 ▢ We do it this way because ...
9 ▢ It works like this.
10 ▢ Just press here.
11 ▢ Do you follow me?
12 ▢ The main reason for this is ...

15

A 20 🔊 At service-drone, potential customers can ask for a demonstration. Listen to Volker explaining the first steps in learning how to fly a drone to Bart, a customer from the Netherlands. What is the most important thing you need to do if you want to fly a drone?

B Look back at the Language focus and listen again. Which of the phrases does Volker use?

C Listen once more, but this time read the transcript on page 92 while you listen. Notice the pauses and stresses Volker uses and how they make it easier to understand the instructions. Practise reading the dialogue with a partner.

Film 2 If you would like to find out more about how drones work, watch the film *Made in Germany*.

Before you watch, turn to the video worksheet on page 106. The exercises will help you make the most of the film.

16

A People give business presentations for different reasons. Match the type of presentation with its purpose and target audience. Can you add any more types of presentations?

1	Briefing	A	to present hard facts to the board of directors
2	Project report	B	to welcome guests or present an award to a large audience
3	Financial report	C	to persuade customers to buy something
4	Sales presentation	D	to give the specific information people need to do their job
5	Technical presentation	E	to update the team or manager on the status of work
6	Talk at special occasion	F	to explain complex issues during a talk at a conference

B Turn back to your notes on business presentations (For the next unit, page 29) and think about the impact of the kind of presentation you are giving on the following questions.

How formal should the talk be?
Do I need to introduce myself/ my company?
How entertaining do I need to be?
How much information do I need to give?
How long should it be?

What kind of presentations do you give or listen to in your job?

17

Language focus: making a presentation easy to follow

It is easier for the audience to follow a presentation if the speaker uses signposting language as a guide.

1 Match the phrases with their purpose in a presentation.

1	Asking for questions	A	Right, let's move on to …
2	Greeting the audience	B	Thank you for your attention.
3	Moving on to the next point	C	So, to sum up …
4	Concluding	D	So let's get started.
5	Introducing the topic	E	We have time for a few questions now.
6	Clarifying a point	F	As I mentioned earlier, …
7	Thanking the audience	G	Good morning everyone. I'd like to welcome you to …
8	Starting the presentation	H	I'd like to cover a number of points and so I'll start with …
9	Referring back or forward	I	In other words, …
10	Explaining the structure	J	As you know, today I'm going to talk about …

2 In which order would you expect to hear the phrases A – J in a presentation? Which phrases might come at more than one stage of a presentation?

At the beginning: G, ______ At the end: ______ At more than one stage: ______

3 Brainstorm other phrases you know which can be used at each stage of a presentation. Turn to **File 26** on page 82 to compare your ideas.

4 Emphasizing the correct words also makes it easier for the audience to follow a presentation. Practise this by reading the phrases A – J aloud.

Knowing signposting language is useful even if you listen to more presentations than you give.

18

The most difficult part of a presentation may be dealing with questions. Practise asking and answering questions on any topic with a partner. Use these expressions to give yourself time to think before you answer.

As I said earlier, … • Well, let me see. • I'm glad you asked that. • That's an interesting point. • Well, this is how I see it. • Where should I start?

19

A Look at this list of choices you have when you give a presentation. What advice would you give? Put a cross on the position on each line which shows your opinion. Then draw a line to join up the crosses.

Give a lot of facts and figures	Tell a lot of stories
Use clear, simple language	Use colourful language
Provide a rational line of argument	Address the emotions of the audience
Get to the point	Introduce your company and yourself in detail
Make your slides simple	Present as much detail as possible on slides
Leave questions to the end	Invite questions at any time

I would always advise someone to …

If you tell a story, that enables you to …

I think it's a good idea to …

B Compare your answers with a partner. How similar are the lines? Can you add any other important points?

20

A One very common piece of advice for presenters is "Know your audience". What should you know about your audience?

B Read some comments about audience expectations from people who work internationally. Which factors from **19A** do they refer to?

The audience will *always* have questions, so allow at least 20 minutes at the end of a talk.
Andrea, Italian working in Brazil

It is more important to give the audience a feeling of who you are rather than what you know.
Mark, German working in China

Audiences don't want to see slides full of text, they prefer listening to the speaker while looking at graphs, tables, diagrams or charts.
Irina, Russian working in Peru

C Choose a country or region from below and find out more about the presentation norms in that country in **File 27** on pages 82 – 83. Work with a partner (preferably someone who chose a different country) and discuss the following questions.

Brazil **France** **Italy** **UAE**
China **India** **Russia** **USA**

1. How do the norms match the advice in **19A** and any other points you added to this list?
2. Would a typical presentation in each country match audience expectations in your own country? Why? Why not?

21

Project work

You are going to give a presentation about the innovative emergency kit developed by WiSMa to potential customers abroad.

1. Choose a country from the country files in **20C** to be your target audience and read about the presentation norms in that country on pages 82 – 83.
2. Read the information about the emergency kit in **File 28** on page 84 and decide what you will include in your presentation.
3. Prepare your presentation in a way you think would make the best impression in the country you chose.
4. Give your presentation. Can your audience guess who the target audience is?

22

Vocabulary: word partnerships

A Choose the correct option to complete each sentence.

1 I must congratulate you on **so / such** an interesting presentation.
2 **Among / Under** other things, you made the audience laugh.
3 That's true, you **definitely / total** have a point there.
4 Do you understand **all this / this all**?
5 Can you help me, please? How does this app **go / work**?

B Use the words below to form word partnerships. Then choose three word partnerships and use them to say something about your company.

advantage • close • environmental • environmentally • maintenance • market • need • reasonable • technology

1 ______ leader
2 ______ relationship
3 innovative ______
4 ______ impact
5 low-______
6 ______ sustainable
7 added ______
8 urgent ______
9 ______ cost

23

Useful language

A "Presentations are better when they sound like a conversation." Do you agree with this statement? Why? Why not?

B 21 Discuss how you can make a presentation sound more conversational. Then listen to two versions of the same presentation. How are they different and which one do you think is more effective for its purpose?

24

Vocabulary: giving advice

Choose one of the situations and advise the person on the best course of action. Use the expressions below, but add ideas of your own. Write down or record the advice you would give.

I've no doubt that ... • I'd suggest that you ... • My reason for suggesting ... is that ... • That would enable you to ... • The best thing would be to ... • It would help if you ...

Situation 1
The son/daughter of one your friends would like to work at your company and has asked you for some advice.

Situation 2
Your colleague has to give a presentation in (choose the country) next month and has asked for advice.

Situation 3
A friend is moving to your region and is looking for somewhere to live. He/She asks you for advice.

Before the next class Make a list of problems companies may have to deal with. Think about any companies you know or have read about. Bring your list to the next class.

For the next unit During the next week, make notes on three phone calls and three emails. Who were you in contact with? What was the purpose of each call/email?

05 Finding solutions

1

A Companies face risks every day. Read the list below and categorize the risks according to how likely you think they are to happen and how serious it would be for your company if they did. Write the letters a – h in the matrix.

Risks:

a A key customer doesn't pay on time.
b A team misses an important deadline.
c Staff go on strike.
d There are major political problems.
e Suppliers don't deliver on time.
f There are problems with the energy supply.
g It is difficult to find staff with the right skills.
h There is conflict within a team.

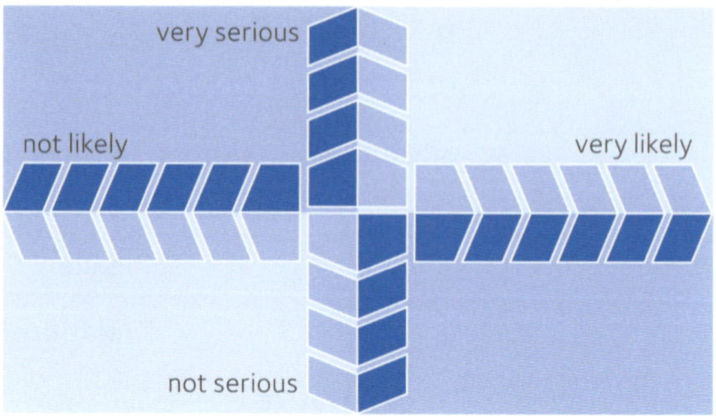

B What else can go wrong? Come up with one additional risk for each square of the matrix.

2

Work with a partner to offer solutions to the issues a – h in **1 A** and to your own ideas (Before the next class, page 37). Use the expressions below to help you.

State the problem:

Offer a solution:

That sounds serious. I think we should ... • Don't worry about that. You can ... • We shouldn't take a risk. Let's ... • Never mind, we can ... • We can solve that problem if we ...

3

Language focus: looking for solutions

If we want to discuss a problem and come up with possible solutions, we often follow a pattern.

A Identifying the reason for the problem:
- *We must have made* a mistake when we changed suppliers.

B Looking back:
- *We should have continued* working with our old suppliers.
- *We shouldn't have closed down* our production plant.
- *They should have hired* professionals to organize the conference.

C Looking forward:
- *We should contact* Mr Nguyen again immediately.

Think back to your dialogues in **2** and suggest what people *should have done* (looking back) and what they *should do* now (looking forward).

4

A Many companies see outsourcing as a good solution. What is your opinion? Should these business activities be outsourced? Which are most often outsourced?

customer support • facility management • invoicing • IT support • manufacturing • marketing • payroll processing • PR • project management • recruitment • secretarial support • software development

Well, it depends on the size of the company. I think ...

I don't think ... should be outsourced because ...

As far as I know, companies often outsource ...

I think companies should concentrate on their core business because ...

core business = main business

B 22 Christopher is the CEO of an IT company based in London. Listen to what he says about his company's outsourcing strategy. Write the terms he uses next to the places on the map.

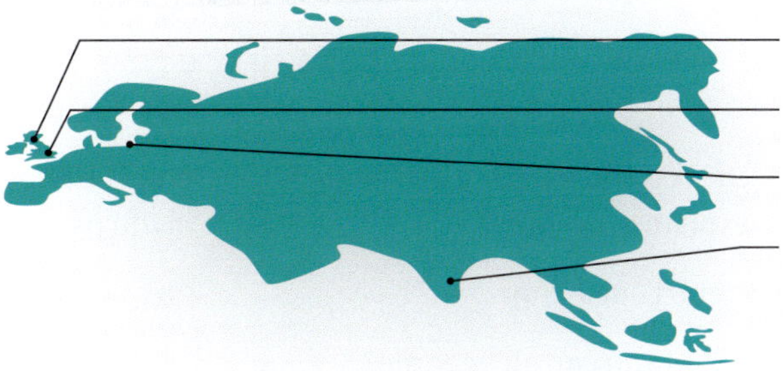

Glasgow: ____________

London: ____________

Gdansk: ____________

Bangalore: *offshoring*

C What jobs do the people in each location do?

What experience do you have of these kinds of outsourcing – at work or as a customer?

5

A Today, countries like Vietnam and Ukraine are competing with traditional outsourcing locations like India and China for projects. Work with a partner to find out what makes them attractive options. Each partner reads about one country and lists the main reasons why that country may be an interesting option for a European IT company. Then compare answers and decide which country is the better option.

Partner A → **File 29**, page 73. **Partner B** → **File 30**, page 78.

Ukraine	Vietnam

B Do you think Christopher, the CEO of the London-based IT company in **4B**, should have chosen to work with partners in Ukraine or in Vietnam? Explain your reasons.

Both countries have ...

Salaries are probably lower in ...

... could have been a better option than ... because ...

One problem in ... may be that ...

6

A What can go wrong during a web meeting or conference call? Look at the pictures and answer the questions.

1 What should the facilitator do now and what should he/she have done earlier?
2 What else could go wrong during meetings like these?

B During a web meeting or conference call, what could you say if you would like to do the following? Sometimes there is more than one correct answer.

a join the meeting
b welcome the participants
c check if the meeting can begin
d explain procedures
e build relationships
f invite participation

1 ▢ Please say your name before you start speaking.
2 ▢ Can I check that everyone is here and you can all hear me?
3 ▢ Can we start with an update from everyone?
4 ▢ By the way, what's the time in Pune, Anaya?
5 ▢ Would you like to comment on this, Andrea?
6 ▢ Hello everyone, it's Jens from Potsdam here.
7 ▢ Please let us know if you have to leave the room.
8 ▢ Thank you all for logging in on time.
9 ▢ I'd like to ask you to mute your microphone when you're not speaking. Thanks.

conference call = concall / confcall / telco

C Which of the sentences 1 – 9 could you also say in a face-to-face meeting? What does this tell us about the differences between face-to-face meetings and virtual meetings?

7

A When you're communicating with people in a virtual meeting or conference call, you can keep everyone focused by asking for comments and checking understanding. Complete these phrases.

concerns • hear • make • mind • position • with

1 Does that ________ sense?
2 What's your ________ on this, Fabio?
3 I'd like to ________ from you, Sonja.
4 Do you have any other ________ ?
5 What's on your ________ , Mike?
6 Is everyone ________ me?

B Which of the questions or statements in **7A** mean:

A ▢ ▢ Tell me your opinion.
B ▢ ▢ Is what I said clear?
C ▢ ▢ Tell me what you are worried about.

8

A Read the agenda of a conference call at a telecommunications company with its headquarters in Paris. Make a note of some words and phrases the participants could say during the call.

Meeting Agenda

Date: 11.03.20.. / Start: 09:00 CET / End: 10:30 CET

Item	Topic	Time allotted	Discussion leader
1	Team updates	15 mins	Erika
2	Customer support portal	20 mins	Amit
3	Rollout of mobile wallet in Nigeria	15 mins	Amaka
4	Open questions about working schedules	15 mins	Camille
5	Next f2f meeting in Mumbai	15 mins	Amit
6	Open questions of the day	10 mins	Erika

rollout / launch = introduction of a new product or service to customers

B 23 Now listen to part of the meeting. Which agenda item are they talking about? Which words give you the answer?

C Listen again and complete what you hear during the meeting.

1 I'm very ______________ the way you managed the rollout in Nigeria.

2 I only received it myself the day ______________ .

3 But let me explain why the schedule ______________ .

4 In other words, we should finish this part of the project ______________ time.

5 I'm sorry, but we can't ______________ for the result.

6 Just to be clear, you mean our deadline is ______________ of April?

7 Yes, but not only that. Could you also ______________ of the discounts you offered?

8 Sorry, could you ______________ , Camille?

D Match each sentence in **8C** with its purpose in the meeting. Then highlight the phrases which show the purpose.

A ☐ to reformulate and repeat some information
B ☐ to clarify a point
C ☐ to make a point strongly / to be firm
D ☐ to add another point
E ☐ to ask someone to repeat what they said
F ☐ to apologize
G ☐ to ask for clarification
H ☐ to motivate and show appreciation

9

Language focus: sorry ...

Match the sentences with their functions. What could you say instead of "sorry" in each case?

1 I'm sorry to hear that you're leaving the team.
2 Sorry, what did you say?
3 I'm sorry, but I don't think that will work.
4 Sorry, I'm late again.
5 Sorry, is this Hall 24?
6 So let's meet again next Tuesday, sorry, I mean next Thursday.

A to apologize
B to correct what you said
C to ask for repetition
D to make your point firmly
E to say you're sad/disappointed
F to attract someone's attention

10

A International expansion allows companies to grow, but it also involves risks. Look at the topics below. Do you think their impact is more likely to be an advantage (+) or a risk (–)?

1 ◯ bureaucracy
2 ◯ company secrets
3 ◯ costs
4 ◯ currency fluctuations
5 ◯ energy supply
6 ◯ language
7 ◯ legal issues
8 ◯ political events
9 ◯ quality control
10 ◯ workforce
11 ◯ working culture

B Do you know if any of the issues above have an impact on your company's international operations?

In …, we have to deal with …

We always expect problems with …

… is very difficult because …

11

Language focus: reporting information

When things go wrong, information has to be passed on quickly. The verb form we choose depends on our message.

A Reporting with no call for action (stating a fact):

1 Enzo *phoned* to say that there *was* a problem at the factory.
2 I *had* a call from Mr Dinh to say that he *was arriving* tomorrow afternoon.

B Reporting with a call for action (saying we should act):

1 Enzo *phoned* to say that *there's* a problem at the factory. Could you please …
2 I *had* a call from Mr Dinh to say that he*'s arriving* tomorrow afternoon. Pick him up …

C Delivering a message:

1 I *got* a text message asking me *to phone* Enzo immediately.

What did each person actually say?

Enzo: "There's ______________________________"

Mr Dinh: "I'm ______________________________"

Sender: "Please ______________________________"

Sometimes we simply summarize what someone says instead of reporting their words.

For example, when someone says:
"Please send me the accident report." or "I'll send you the report tomorrow."
→ You could summarize the request by saying *(Name) contacted me about the accident report.*

"Please let me know what happened." or "How serious was it?"
→ You could summarize the question with *I emailed her to ask about the accident.*

12

Think about your own recent email correspondence and phone calls and complete the sentences. Show them to a partner and give him / her some more details.

1 … phoned me to tell/ask me …
2 … emailed me to say that …
3 I contacted … about …
4 I emailed … to remind him/her to …

13

A Have you ever noticed that your international partners and colleagues often have different preferences when it comes to communication? Read what Angélica from Querétaro says about this.

> In Mexico, instead of sending emails or using instant messaging, people like to come to your office to talk. If we're working at different locations, we prefer to call people as this shows that we value their answer. If you just send an email about an important matter which you haven't discussed by phone or in person before, people will think that you're rude. That's why it's common to discuss something and then send an email as a confirmation. I work for a Canadian company in Mexico and some Canadian colleagues, based here and in Canada, have told me that they prefer to use email or IM because it takes less time!

B 24 Listen to colleagues from three different countries talking about their communication preferences and the norms in their countries. Make notes on where the speakers come from, their preferred way of communicating and their reasons for this. Who do you think would find it easy to work together?

14

A For many reasons, emails are probably the most popular channel of communication in international business. Read and compare these two emails. Then answer the questions below.

email A

Dear Ms ...

I'd like to remind you of the request I sent you a few weeks ago (see attachment) as I haven't received an answer from you yet. It would be a pity if your company profile could not be included in our publication as it reaches a wide audience in your sector.

I look forward to your feedback by the end of this week so that we can draft a text and send it to you for your approval.

Sincerely

...

email B

Dear Ms ...

I would like to congratulate you on your excellent presentation at the conference last week. It must have generated a lot of new business for the company, so I'm sure you're very busy right now.

Unfortunately, I didn't have the chance to speak to you in person at the conference, so I'm writing today to ask for an overview of your company's operations for our publication. You'll find a checklist of the kind of information we need in the attachment. In order to save you time, we will draft a text and send it to you for your approval.

If possible, please send the details by the end of the week because we would like to include your company profile in our publication.

Looking forward to hearing from you.

Best wishes

...

1. What is the purpose of the emails? Underline the words which give you the answer.
2. Emails are usually either topic-focused or people-focused. What examples of this difference can you find in these two emails?
3. Which one is closer to the kind of emails you receive or write in your company?

B What could the writer of each email be thinking?

The writer of email A/B thinks ...

"I need an answer very quickly."
"She is so inefficient."
"She must be very busy."
"I'll just send a quick email to remind her."
"The request is not important, so if she doesn't answer ..."
"I don't want to sound too impatient."

C With a partner, write replies to email A and email B in the style of the original emails. Compare your emails with another pair and discuss any differences.

15

A What effect could these aspects have on the style of written business communication?

content • cultural norms • frequency of communication • reason for writing • relationship with the recipient • stage in relationship

B Read this email exchange between Spanish (Cristina and Miriam) and British (Adam, Jessica and Joe) colleagues. Then, discuss the questions. All the emails were written on the same day.

email 1

To: Joe
CC: Cristina

Dear Joe,

I hope you are well. Cristina is looking for some data (number of accounts, number of coupons downloaded, etc.) for the mobile wallet for the first months after its rollout. Do you have any numbers for the first year?

If not, could you please tell us who may have this information?

Thanks in advance.

Kind regards,
Miriam

email 2

To: Adam; Jessica
CC: Miriam; Cristina

Adam / Jessica,

See request below from Miriam / Cristina, regarding stats for the mobile wallet for the first year.

Is this something either of you could help with?

Thanks,
Joe

email 3

To: Joe; Jessica; Miriam
CC: Cristina; Leo; Simon

Looping in Leo who may also be able to help. Leo produces a weekly/ monthly report on wallet numbers/stats ... Think there's also an activity report produced by the Product Mgmt team – Simon?

Miriam – I think you'll need to draw up a list of which data points you want to send to Jessica / Leo.

A.

email 4

To: Joe; Jessica; Adam; Cristina

Cristina, could you please send them a list with the information you need?

Thanks to all for your collaboration.

Kind regards,
Miriam

email 5

To: Miriam; Joe; Jessica; Adam
CC: Leo; Simon

Hello all,

I would be grateful if you could please provide any available info related to our mobile wallet, specifically for the first months of life such as:

– # of users (registered and active users)
– # of users with at least 1 payment card
– Type of payment card
– Average prepaid price of purchased coupon

Thanks and best regards,
Cristina

1 What did you notice about the communication styles?
2 What did you notice about the language used by the Spanish and British colleagues?
3 Underline the phrases you would use in your own emails.

Discuss similarities or differences with your own work emails.

16

Project work

Create a list of useful phrases often used in written communication.

1 Discuss these questions about the written communication in your department.
   a Who do you write to in English?
   b What do you write about?
   c How formal/informal is the communication?
   d How technical is the content?

2 Based on your answers to the questions above and your notes (For the next unit, page 37), start to make a list of useful expressions. Do this in English or in your own language.

3 Share your list with the group and choose the 10 most useful phrases. Group the phrases according to their function (e.g. starting an email) and, if necessary, find English equivalents.

17 Listening: reporting information

25 Listen to excerpts from four telephone calls. How would you pass on the information from them to someone else? Listen again and write down what you could say. There may be more than one possible answer, so explain your choices.

18 Vocabulary: fixed expressions

Complete the first part of the phrases with the words below. Then finish each sentence in any way you like.

after • far • mean • words • wrong

1 What's ______________? Oh, we had a problem ...
2 In other ______________, you think ...
3 How about the day ______________ tomorrow? We could ...
4 I see what you ______________. So what do you ...
5 As ______________ as I know, there was ...

19 Useful language

A What would you say in each situation?

a you want to start a conference call ______________
b you want to check if people understand ______________
c you think something is wrong ______________
d you want some input from others ______________
e you want to get someone's attention ______________
f you want to praise someone ______________

B Match the phrases below to the situations in **19A**.

1 ☐ Does that make sense?
2 ☐ Can I hear your opinion on this?
3 ☐ That's very impressive.
4 ☐ Can I check that you're all here and that everyone can hear me?
5 ☐ What's the matter?
6 ☐ Sorry, could I ask you something?

Before the next class What big or small changes have taken place in your company recently? Try to find some statistics and bring the information to the next class.

For the next unit Do visitors from abroad visit your company? Find out where they are from, the reasons for their visits and who deals with them.

06 Hosting visitors

1

A Do you think companies have increased or reduced the money they spend on business travel in recent years? Elano from Brazil, Yang from China, Haruto from Japan, Darya from Russia and Scott from the USA were asked about their companies' spending. Look at these results and decide which country you think the figures refer to.

Business travel spending (in %)

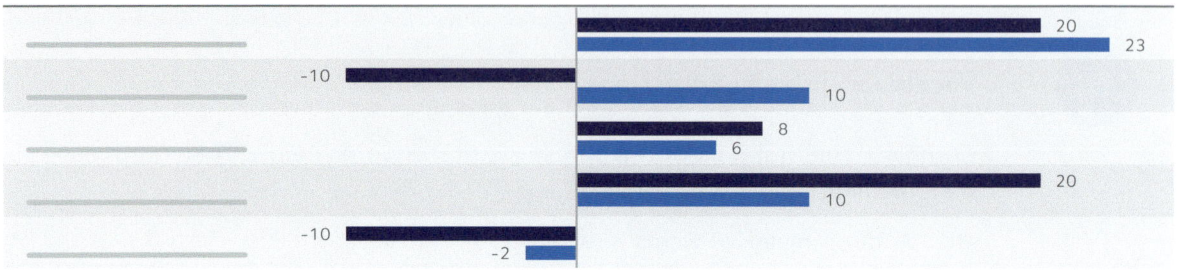

26 Listen to what they say and confirm or correct your answers.

B Choose a word to make the sentences match the information in **1A**.

1 Elano's company **increased / reduced** spending in 2015.
2 Spending in Yang's company **rose slightly / fell sharply** in 2015.
3 Haruto thinks he can see a(n) **upward / downward** trend in his company's travel spending.
4 Darya says that the number of business trips has **increased sharply / remained the same**.
5 Spending in Scott's company was **higher / lower** in 2015 than in 2014.

2

A Read the statements and complete the graphs.

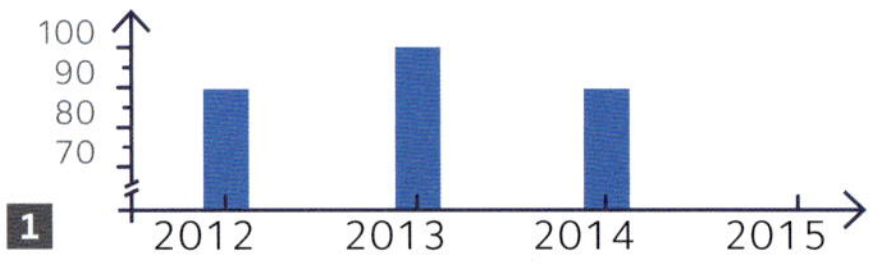

The number of business trips **fell by** 10 % in 2015.

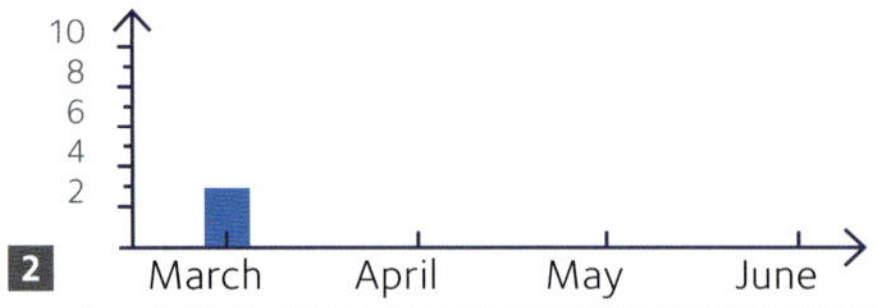

Our use of virtual meetings **has increased steadily from** three per month in March **to** ten in June.

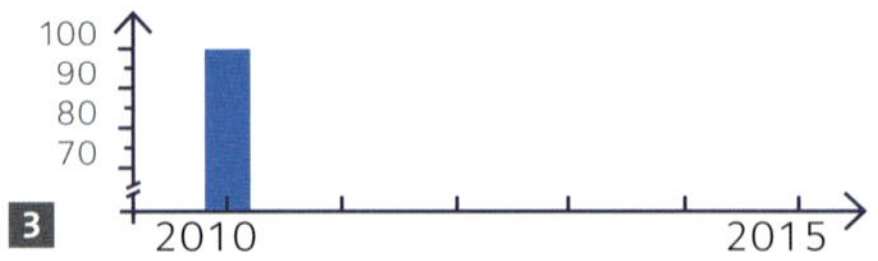

The number of visits by our Chinese partners **has fallen by** 20 % from 2010 to 2015.

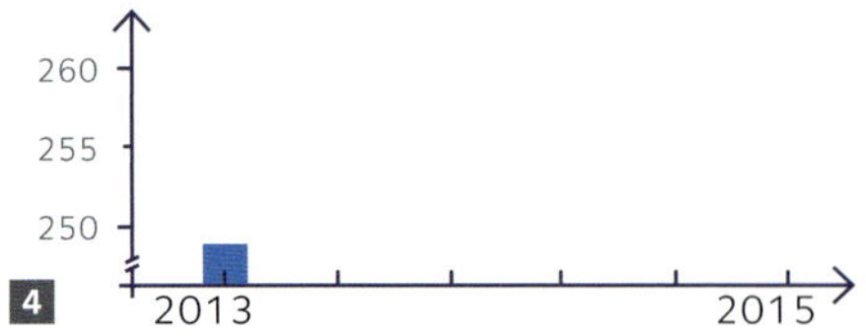

Between 2013 and 2015, the size of our workforce **increased slightly from** 250 **to** 255.

B What did you find out about the changes in your company or your department (Before the next class, page 45)? Use the phrases in **1B** and the highlighted words in **2A** to help you talk about them. Add your own ideas.

in the past = numbers ***fell*** *last year*
up to now = numbers ***have fallen*** *this year*

3

A Why do people travel on business? Think of as many reasons as you can.

B **27** Peter is talking about business travel in his company. Listen and answer the questions.

1 What are the main reasons for Peter's business trips?
- 1 ☐ to visit customers
- 2 ☐ to attend trade fairs
- 3 ☐ to go to conferences
- 4 ☐ to visit and find new suppliers

2 Which statement summarizes what he says about his own business travel activities?
- 1 ☐ The reduced travel budget means that he travels less now.
- 2 ☐ He is less affected by the spending cuts than many of his colleagues.
- 3 ☐ Visiting his suppliers is the only way to bring results for his company.

C Virtual communication is becoming more and more popular. So, from a company's point of view, is it worth spending a lot of money on business travel? Complete the sentence with your own opinion.

It's (not) worth spending a lot of money on business trips because …

4

Language focus: presenting a convincing argument

1 Match the sentences 1 – 10 with the stage in the process a – e.

- a expressing an opinion
- b providing supporting arguments
- c referring to other points of view
- d reformulating
- e summarizing

1 ☐ *An added benefit is that* we can develop a personal relationship.
2 ☐ *So what I'm trying to say is* that we should rethink our strategy.
3 ☐ *I'm convinced that* we should reduce our spending on business trips.
4 ☐ *So in other words*, I think we should go ahead as planned.
5 ☐ *All things considered*, it looks as if we should change our policy slightly.
6 ☐ *I'm aware that* not everyone agrees with me on this.
7 ☐ *Another standpoint is* that face-to-face meetings increase sales.
8 ☐ *If you ask me*, we made the right decision.
9 ☐ *And what's more*, we also save a lot of time.
10 ☐ *So to sum up* the discussion so far, …

2 **28** Listen to a manager from the USA talking about business travel. What is his point of view? What is his most convincing argument in your opinion?

3 Listen again. Underline the phrases in *italics* above which he uses. In what order does he use the phrases and what reason could he have for choosing this order?

5

A Work with a partner. Partner A makes a list of arguments for face-to-face meetings and Partner B makes a list of arguments for virtual meetings. Compare and discuss your lists. Use phrases from **4** to help you.

B After listening to your partner's arguments, has your opinion on business travel changed from what you wrote in **3C**? Explain your point of view.

6

Who comes to your company from abroad and why do they come? Refer to your notes (For the next unit, page 45).

As far as I know, ...

Well, in my depart-ment we get foreign visitors ...

Most foreign visitors at our company come to ...

We don't get many visitors from abroad because ...

7

A Peter is meeting the head of a logistics company from the Netherlands for the first time. If you were the host, what would you say to your guest in each situation? Write down your ideas and compare your answers with a partner.

a ◯ greeting

b ◯ getting a security pass

c ◯ showing them where things are

d ◯ chatting while walking along a corridor

e ◯ knocking on an office door

f ◯ looking at a schedule

B **29** Now listen to what Peter says in each situation. Match the phrases 1–6 you hear to the photos a–f above.

C Discuss in class your answers to **7A** and what Peter says and note down at least two new phrases you could use in each situation.

Film 3 If you would like to find out more about meeting business partners from abroad, watch the film *In my experience*.

Before you watch, turn to the video worksheet on page 108. The exercises will help you make the most of the film.

8

A How important do you think it is to use words like *please* and *thank you* when you want to sound polite? Are there any other words or expressions you think are necessary?

B Decide whether these short dialogues are impolite, polite or over-polite. Compare your choices in class. If you chose impolite or over-polite, what would you say if you were the speaker?

	impolite	polite	over-polite
1 The speaker is returning a missed call from an unknown person. Speaker: "Who call?"	▢	▢	▢
2 The speaker is talking to a colleague he/she knows quite well. Speaker: "I'm going to a bar this evening. Do you want to come or not?"	▢	▢	▢
3 The speaker is asking a colleague to check a document. Speaker: "You couldn't have a look at this for a second, could you?"	▢	▢	▢
4 The speaker is replying to the question "Can you send me the report this afternoon, please?" Speaker: "Of course."	▢	▢	▢

C Would you change your mind about the answers you gave in **8B** if …

1 you didn't know the colleague very well (dialogue 2)?
2 the colleague had a higher position than you in the company (dialogue 3)?
3 your boss was asking you (dialogue 4)?

D Work with a partner to find out what people from different countries say about how polite they think the sentences in **8B** are. Read your file and exchange the information. Does what you find out make you change your mind about your answers in **8B**?

Partner A → **File 31**, page 73. **Partner B** → **File 32**, page 78.

9

A Look at this picture. Imagine you are Julie and decide how you would answer Jim's question in two of these situations.

- Jim is Julie's boss
- Julie is a new employee
- Jim and Julie have worked together for five years
- the conversation takes place in the corridor
- Jim has come over to Julie's desk

B Compare your answers in class. How many different answers are there?

C Read about Marco's experience in a café in Berlin. Do you agree with Marco? If so, what could the waitress have said or done? If you disagree with him, what should he have said or done instead?

> I'd only just arrived in Berlin from Hong Kong and I went to meet Chih-Wei, my friend from Taiwan, in a café. We sat down and I got out my laptop because I wanted to show my friend something. I couldn't get online, so I asked the waitress for the access code. Do you know what she said? "I'm sorry you can't have it. We don't want people spending hours in here working or on Facebook." I couldn't believe my ears. How rude!

D Do you think it's more polite to be honest or tactful? Before you discuss this question, read Marco's German friends' explanation and what Chih-Wei thinks a waitress in Taiwan would probably have said in **File 33** on page 84.

10

A Business visitors often bring small gifts for their hosts. Look at these three examples that different visitors have bought and answer the questions.

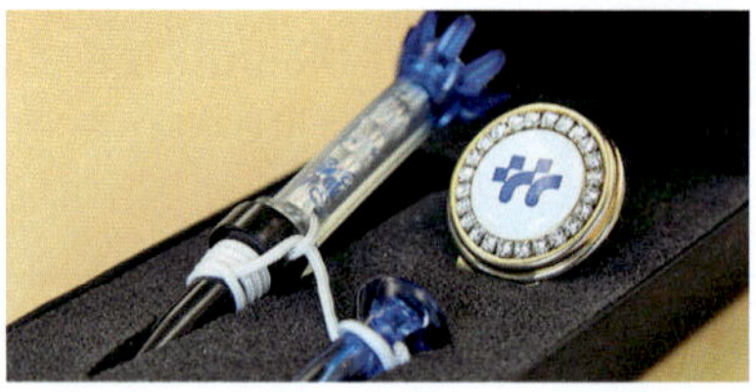

1 Why do you think the visitors chose each gift?
2 How would you react if you were presented with each one?
3 What would you say in each case?

30 Now listen to what was actually said in the three gift-giving scenarios.

B Think of a gift you would give a business partner. Role-play your own exchange of gifts.

11

Language focus: talking about rules and preferences

1 Read about gift-giving protocol in different countries. Which refer to **a** rules and **b** preferences?

1 ☐ In China, a business gift must be given to a department or company, never to an individual.
2 ☐ In most companies in the USA, staff are not allowed to accept gifts worth more than $25.
3 ☐ Business associates in Portugal exchange gifts as a sign of respect, and they can't be refused. That would be very rude.
4 ☐ In Singapore, government officials are not allowed to accept gifts.
5 ☐ In countries like Japan and Indonesia, gift-giving is a tradition, so you have to take gifts for your business partners there.

2 Does your company have rules on these topics? What are they?

Accepting gifts • Security • Dress code/Protective clothing

12

A Make mini-dialogues by matching the questions or statements with a suitable response.

1 Oh, that looks delicious. Is it a local specialty?
2 Please have some more.
3 So, shall I drive you back to the hotel?
4 Would you like another drink?
5 Maybe we can discuss this further over dinner.
6 Thanks for making us feel so welcome.
7 Do you have children?
8 So, we're meeting again at 9 am tomorrow. OK?

A Yes, two. Anyway, I think the taxi's waiting for us.
B Well, I'm busy now, so how about tomorrow?
C Oh, I can't. I'm really full, thanks.
D It was a pleasure to have you here.
E Right, I have the schedule here.
F Well, it has been a very long day.
G That sounds like a good idea. But this one is on me.
H Yes, in fact it's our national dish.

B When or where do you think each dialogue takes place?

C 31 Now listen to the dialogues to check your answers to **12A**. Pay attention to the intonation of the sentences.

13

A Imagine that a group of business partners are visiting your company for three days. Where would they eat their meals?

a in your company canteen
b at a small local restaurant
c in an expensive restaurant
d at your home
e in the office with a buffet provided by a catering service

Well, at lunchtime, I would ...

On one evening at least, they would ...

B What would you say? Match the sentences 1–8 to the situations a–e in **13A**. There may be more than one possible answer. Can you add any more phrases?

1 Please help yourself.
2 Shall I ask for an English menu?
3 The trays are over there.
4 This one is a local speciality.
5 I'd recommend this one.
6 Don't bother reading today's menu, just come and have a look.
7 We come here often.
8 Shall I tell you what we're having?

speciality UK / specialty US

C Read two anecdotes about business meals in **File 34** on page 84. Discuss what went wrong in each case with a partner. What should you consider when inviting visitors from other countries for a meal?

Share any similar experiences you have had with the group.

14

Language focus: vague language

Sometimes we are asked to explain things we're not sure about. In this case, we often use vague language. Here are some examples of ways of describing items on a menu:

- Before it's cooked, it looks *a bit like* a potato.
- As far as I know, it's *a kind of* cabbage.
- That one tastes *something like* baklava to me.
- I read somewhere that the taste is very *similar to* an apple.
- It's a cream dessert or *something like that*.
- It's *a sort of* curry, but it's not Thai or Indian *or anything*.
- I think this is *a type of* Irish bread.
- It's a tomato-*like* fruit, but it's orange in colour.

What are the following? If you don't know, just guess using the vague language.

1 What is a rambutan? 2 What is boorsoq? 3 What are alfajores? 4 What is bobotie?

The answers are in **File 35** on page 85.

15

A 32 Listen to descriptions of special dishes from four different countries and match them to the pictures below. Which one would you prefer to eat?

B Imagine you are taking a foreign visitor to your company canteen or a local restaurant. How would you explain some of the things on the menu to him/her?

16

A If you were responsible for entertaining business visitors, where would you take them? How much time would you expect to spend with them?

to a restaurant • to a sports event • to a museum or art gallery • to a scenic spot • to a local historical site • to the theatre • to do some (active) sport • to a karaoke bar • to your home • to a shopping centre

Your answer may be *It depends*. If so, what does it depend on?

B Read how some other people answered these questions. Which answer is closest to yours?

I take visitors to eat typical local food, usually fish or elk meat. Finns enjoy outdoor sports, but I don't usually invite guests to do any active sport unless I know they are keen on it. I always take them to the Pyyniki park, there's a wonderful view over the city and the two lakes from the tower there. First of all, though, I always ask if they would like time to themselves.
Tarja, Tampere

When we have foreign guests, we always plan a busy schedule of banquets, visiting scenic spots and shopping. There are many interesting historical sites in the city. One place our visitors always enjoy is the Giant Panda Research Centre. It's world-famous. Chengdu is well-known in China for being a relaxing place to visit.
Wang Ping, Chengdu

Regular socializing after work with colleagues is very common in Japan, and our visitors enjoy that too. We take our visitors to good restaurants and bars in the Umeda area. Especially if we have female visitors, we take them to karaoke bars. It's unusual to invite a business partner to your home, but it can happen if the relationship is close.
Akio, Osaka

We usually organize one dinner in a nice restaurant and take our visitors to some kind of event. It depends on their interests, so we always ask them what they would like to do. We have a very good art museum here, for example. Many visitors enjoy a tour of the football stadium, and if there's a match on while they're here, we get tickets for them.
Simon, Wolfsburg

C Think of a place such as a building, a monument or a scenic spot in your area which could be of interest to visitors. What would you tell them about it?

It was built in …

It's a bit controversial because …

This is unique because …

It's used for …

It's one of the most famous …

People come here because …

It has the largest collection of …

17

Project work
You are going to plan the entertainment for a delegation of four visitors to your company. The visitors have come for meetings, but will be free on four evenings and for one half-day.

1 Decide on the country or countries they come from.
2 Plan a social programme for them. Think about the following questions:
   a What places in your area will you show them?
   b What will you tell them about the places?
   c If they want to buy souvenirs, what will you suggest?
   d What evening activities will you plan?

Now role-play the situation. Greet your visitors and explain the programme to them. Another group will play the role of your visitors.

18 Vocabulary: introductions

Imagine you are meeting a business partner for the first time. How would you explain what your position is? Use the same framework as Peter (page 47, **3B**) to talk about yourself.

As a/the … I'm responsible for …, so I …

… is important, so I … . This is a good way to …

19 Useful language

"All companies with international contacts should use English as their working language." Do you agree or disagree? Develop a convincing argument using phrases from the Language focus on page 47 to help you. Use this structure:

State your opinion:	Give supporting arguments:	Refer to other points of view:	Reformulate:	Summarize:

20 Listening: a business dinner

A 33 Listen to three short conversations. What is the purpose of each one? Choose from the functions and match the letters to the conversations.

a accepting
b asking for advice
c thanking
d inviting
e offering
f ordering
g paying
h recommending
i refusing
j suggesting
k commenting on the food

Conversation 1: b, ________

Conversation 2: ________

Conversation 3: ________

B Who would probably say this: **a** the guest or **b** the host?

1 ☐ Shall I pick you up at the hotel?
2 ☐ Yes, that's a good choice.
3 ☐ I'm not sure what to have. What are you having?
4 ☐ I'll just ask for the bill.
5 ☐ Well, it's been a very nice evening.

Before the next class Take some photographs of your office or prepare to describe it. What changes would you like to make?

For the next unit What do you like best about your job? Talk to three people you know who don't work in your company. Ask them this question and note down what they say.

07 Cooperating effectively

1

A *Get Britain Standing* is a campaign to improve the health and productivity of employees. Look at the statistics and discuss the questions.

Get Britain Standing.org™

1 Is there a similar organization in your own country?
2 Have you ever thought that sitting for long periods is bad for you?
3 Could you do your work standing up or walking? Would you want to?
4 Do you think you would get very tired if you stood at your desk?
5 If you believe exercise is good for you, would you prefer to
   a stand and walk more at work or   b sit at work and be active after work?
6 Do you know of any companies which encourage office staff to stand and walk while working?

A
In Britain, the 4.9 m sick days caused by work-related back pain cost companies £5bn per year.

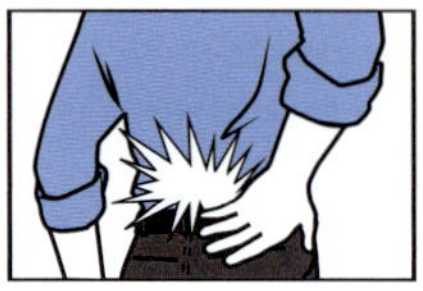

B
70 % of our "sitting time" is at work. We sit for 66 % – 75 % of our working time.

C
- 90 % of Scandinavian office workers have sit-stand desks.
- In the UK, less than 1 % of the office workers have sit-stand desks.
- 80 % of the people who try sit-stand desks want to continue using them.

D
- Productivity at your desk increases by 10 % – 20 % when you stand.
- 62 % of people say they're happier when they alternate between sitting and standing.

Based on: www.getbritainstanding.org

B How long do you sit on an average day? Answer the questionnaire and compare your results in class.

1	Eating (breakfast, lunch, dinner, etc.)	____ hours	____ minutes
2	Commuting	____ hours	____ minutes
3	Working (at your workplace and at home)	____ hours	____ minutes
4	Relaxing (watching TV, surfing the internet, socializing, etc.)	____ hours	____ minutes

Are you surprised by the results? Do your results match those in statistic B above?

2

A Read two comments about making meetings more effective. Do you do these things in your company? Discuss whether you think they are good ideas.

"We removed the tables and chairs from our meeting rooms. Now our meetings are much shorter and more effective. Nobody wastes time."

"Walking meetings save us from PowerPoint! We've noticed that we get our best ideas during such meetings. To make them successful, we only have one or two items on the agenda, ban smartphones and plan a few minutes of desk time at the end to clarify any questions."

B Brainstorm as many ways as you can to stand and move more at work. Then turn to **File 36** on page 85 to compare your ideas. What is your opinion on the suggestions? Which of the things on the list do you do?

3

Read some comments from staff from different companies about their working environment. Compare them with your own situation (Before the next class, page 53).

1 "It's always very difficult to book a meeting room. We just don't have enough of them."
2 "I share an office with three other colleagues, so there's always someone speaking on the phone."
3 "We have just one central printer for everyone, and I have to walk five minutes to get to it."
4 "I'm only in my office for two days a week on average."

We're lucky because … | *… is a problem here too. We …* | *It's different in our company. Here …*

4

A **34** Listen to Ali, a workplace design consultant in Germany, talking about activity-based working (ABW) and how it can help companies and staff work more effectively. In which order does Ali talk about these aspects of activity based working?

- ☐ cost-saving
- ☐ innovation potential
- ☐ productivity
- ☐ staff well-being

B Listen to the first part of Ali's explanation again and complete the gaps.

1 Companies can't always find employees with the skills they need ______ they have to make the working environment more attractive.

2 Many offices are designed for two activities – sitting at a desk or sitting in a meeting. ______ a lack of flexibility.

3 Providing this flexibility ______ give up their own fixed workstation.

4 This freedom of choice ______ better job satisfaction.

5

Language focus: fact-finding questions

Ali mentions that the first step to designing the best company layout is to ask staff how they use space and resources. Complete the questions using the words below. Then make up questions of your own about a typical working week and ask a partner.

far • long • many • much • often

1 How ______ are you in the office?
2 How ______ files do you actively use each day?
3 How ______ of your work requires close concentration?
4 How ______ away are the colleagues you work with regularly?
5 How ______ do you spend on the phone?

6

A Work with a partner to find out more about the pros and cons of activity-based working. Use the information in the files, what you heard from Ali and your own ideas to explain the effects of the changes ABW requires.

Partner A → **File 37**, page 73. **Partner B** → **File 38**, page 79.

Flexible working leads to …

The lack of fixed workstations means that …

B Would you implement ABW in your company? Look back at your answers to **4** and **6A**. With a partner who agrees with you, choose the best arguments to justify your opinion to the class.

7

A Look at the mind map of the 3Ps of communication. Who is communicating (people), where (place) and why (purpose)? Circle all the aspects which reflect your own work. Can you think of any more? Brainstorm as many ideas as possible.

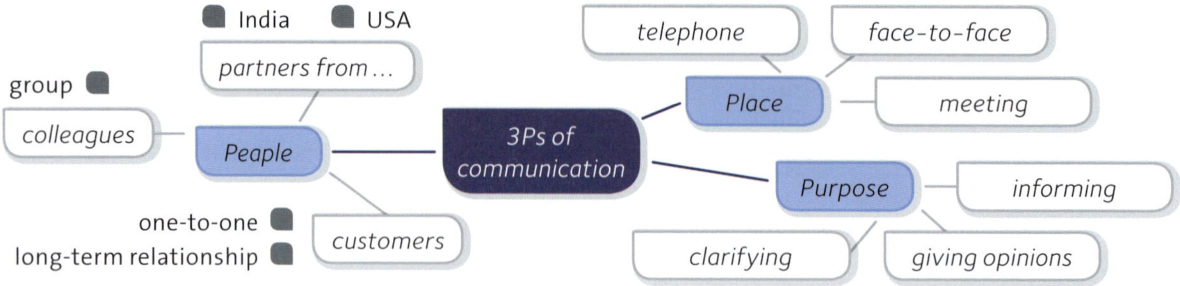

B Vitaly works as a consultant in a Swiss IT company which specializes in identity management solutions for global corporations. He has written a profile of the kind of communicative events he deals with, based on the mind map. Write your own profile in the same format.

People	Place	Purpose	Phrases for performing the task
client colleague project manager supplier	telephone virtual meeting face-to-face email	greeting ending a conversation / an email making arrangements changing arrangements	
client colleague supplier	telephone email virtual meeting	asking for information clarifying understanding asking for repetition	
colleague project manager team members	face-to-face telephone	asking for advice briefing checking understanding	

8

A 35 Listen to Vitaly and match the numbers of the things he says 1 – 5 to the examples of tasks from his communication profile a – e.

a ☐ asking a colleague for advice on the telephone

b ☐ changing arrangements on the telephone with a new supplier

c ☐ greeting a client he knows well at a face-to-face meeting

d ☐ making a telephone call to a client with an urgent question

e ☐ clarifying understanding at a meeting with a client

B Listen again and write down the phrases he uses to perform each task.

C Look at excerpts from two of Vitaly's emails. Match them to sections of his communication profile in **7B**. Who do you think he is writing to? Why do you think that?

1 I'd be grateful if you could send me the specifications at your earliest convenience.

2 Just give me a call if you need any more info.
Cheers
V.

__Cheers__ is used in informal communication. It can mean __thanks__, __goodbye__, __hello__ and __no problem__. It is also used as a toast when you drink with someone.

9

Language focus: requesting and inquiring

We often use the past progressive if a request is a big favour and/or if we're speaking to someone of higher status. We don't normally use it for simple requests.

Asking for a big favour:
- I was wondering if you could offer us a discount.
- I was hoping that we could discuss this now.
- I was thinking that we could move our meeting forward to next week.

Simple request:
Could you lend me your pen? (~~I was wondering if you could lend me your pen.~~)

It's a good idea to add a reason before you actually ask for a favour.

Add a reason:
- As we've been business partners for so long now, I was wondering if ...
- Our project deadline is very soon, so I was hoping that ...
- Olga told me that you are going to Paris on Thursday, so I was thinking that ...

Role-play two conversations with a partner. Use the role-cards in **File 39** on page 85 or your own ideas.

10

A These expressions are often used when people make arrangements to meet. Replace the underlined part of each sentence with the term which has the same meaning.

a call off • **b** get together • **c** make it • **d** put off • **e** take it further

1 ☐ I'd like to <u>discuss this a bit more with you</u>. How about going for lunch?
2 ☐ We can't <u>postpone</u> the meeting again!
3 ☐ I'm afraid we're going to have to <u>cancel</u> the meeting.
4 ☐ This is a difficult situation, so I was thinking we should <u>meet in person</u> to discuss it.
5 ☐ I was wondering if you could <u>come</u> on Friday?

B 36 Now listen to four telephone conversations. What are the speakers doing in each one?

a ☐ They're making a possible but not fixed arrangement.
b ☐ They're making vague arrangements.
c ☐ They're changing existing arrangements.
d ☐ They can't find a time to meet.

C Here are some of the sentences you heard in **10B**. The underlined words are stressed. Choose the most suitable question in each case.

1 a ☐ Do you want me to phone you or shall we get together?
b ☐ What do you want to discuss?
– I'd prefer to <u>meet</u> to discuss the campaign.

2 a ☐ Are you sure Tuesday suits you?
b ☐ Which day suits you better?
– Yes, I <u>think</u> I can make it on Tuesday.

3 a ☐ Shall we meet at ten?
b ☐ Does that give you enough time to get to the airport?
– That will give me <u>plenty</u> of time.

4 a ☐ How are you getting home?
b ☐ When are you leaving the conference?
– I'm driving home <u>straight after</u> the last talk.

If you stress the correct words, it's easier for others to understand you.

11

A To get a positive answer to a request, we often start by saying *I know …, but …* . Complete each request with your own ideas.

For example: I know it's late, but *could you email me the latest figures before you go home?*

1 I know it's expensive, but ______

2 I know it's short notice, but ______

3 I know you're very busy, but ______

4 I know this is a difficult question, but ______

B With a partner, choose one of the requests as a starting point and make up a dialogue.

12

A Think about the following situations and decide what you would say in each case. Make up any reasons or other details you need. Compare your ideas with a partner.

Situation 1 Your colleague has arranged to meet a client for dinner and asks you to come too. You refuse.
Situation 2 In a meeting, your colleagues suggest a way to speed up the project schedule. You disagree.

B **37** Listen to three short sequences from a meeting to discuss the introduction of activity-based working. Which statement is true?

1 ☐ Rosa signals agreement. ☐ Rosa signals disagreement.

2 ☐ Ben accepts the request. ☐ Ben refuses the request.

3 ☐ Claudia responds positively. ☐ Claudia responds negatively.

C Listen again and read the transcript on page 98. As you listen, underline the phrases which gave you the answers in **12B**. Practise reading the short dialogues with a partner.

13

Match the phrases which have the same purpose in a conversation.

1	I see your point, but ...	A	Thank you, but I have to say no.
2	Oh, by the way ...	B	The deadline is next week, so please ...
3	I'm afraid it's against company policy, so ...	C	Exactly!
4	Really? Are you sure about that?	D	Before I forget ...
5	That's a very good point.	E	That's one way of looking at it, but ...
6	We need a decision, so could you ...	F	Do you really think so?

14

Language focus: guiding your listeners

We can help people follow what we are saying by using short "signposting" words. What is the function of each expression in **bold**? Choose from the suggestions below.

a to change the topic • **b** to end a conversation • **c** to start a conversation • **d** to give permission • **e** to show you are thinking • **f** to attract attention • **g** to move on to the next point

1 ☐ A: **Oh**, could I have a look at your newspaper for a minute? ☐ B: **Of course**. Go ahead.
2 ☐ A: How was the meeting? ☐ B: **Well**, it's hard to say. We talked about ...
3 ☐ **OK**, let's have a look at the sales figures now.
4 ☐ **Anyway**, to get back to what I was saying.
5 ☐ **Right**. Jan, can we start with the results of your survey?
6 ☐ **So**, I'll see you all again next week.

15

A When you speak in English to people from different countries, what makes communication difficult? Look at the results of a survey of students studying in an international group in Berlin and discuss whether you share their opinions.

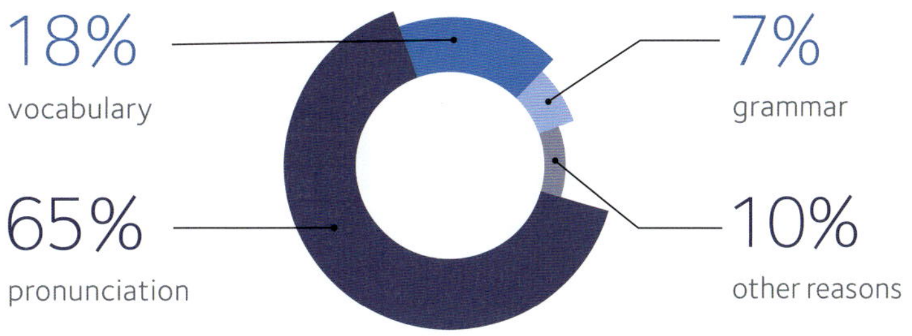

B Does your answer to the question in **15 A** depend on the first language of the people you are communicating with? How important is the medium of communication? Read these comments and compare them with your own experience.

When I started working with my Spanish colleague, we found it difficult to understand each other. I know a Glaswegian accent is not the easiest to understand! Now we've got used to each other's accents, so there are no more problems.

Alistair, Glasgow

I have no difficulty communicating in English with my German business partners. I suppose it's because our native languages are similar.

Thijs, Amsterdam

I'm working on a multi-national project, and the biggest problem we all have is speaking on the phone. Pronunciation becomes a real issue if you don't see the person you're speaking to.

Alena, Prague

Take advantage of the millions of videos on YouTube to listen and get used to people speaking English with different accents.

16

A Which English sounds do you find most difficult to say? Do you think this makes it hard for other people to understand you?

B 38 Listen to Marchién from the Netherlands, Hannes from Austria, Yamato from Japan and Sandrine from France and write down what they say. How is their pronunciation different from standard English? Could this cause misunderstandings?

17

A Read what Gabriel says and discuss how you can show that you are motivated to understand other people's English.

When we work internationally, it is critical that we are willing and able to interact with many different kinds of people from diverse language backgrounds and look for common ground.

Gabriel, Monterrey, Mexico

B Role-play two situations in which you and your partner have problems understanding each other.

Partner A → **File 40**, page 74. **Partner B** → **File 41**, page 79.

C Which role-play was more successful? Why? Compare the phrases in the files and discuss which ones lead to more successful communication.

18

A You are going to hear part of two interviews from a survey on job satisfaction. The two interviewees are Filipe, a business development manager at Sozé Shoes, and Manish, a yoga teacher and owner of yoga centres. Which terms do you think you will hear in each interview? Could any of the words come up in both interviews?

physically exhausting · popular activities · sense of satisfaction · buyers · personal contact · senior citizens · positive effect · people-centred · booth · latest collection · target client · different parts of the world · trade fair · production capacity · family · digital experience

B 39 Listen and make notes on the answers to the survey questions in the table below. Don't try to note down every word.

	Filipe from Sozé Shoes	Manish from Total Yoga
What is the most important part of your job?		
What is the hardest part of your job?		
What do you enjoy most?		
What's one of the best things about your job?		
What do you enjoy least about your job?		

C What about you? Answer the questions in the table about your own job.

19

Filipe and Manish both talk about aspects of their job where they interact with people. What are the similarities and differences in the kind of interactions they are talking about? Think about the 3Ps: people, place and purpose.

Both of them ...

... gives instructions so that ...

... explains how ...

... asks his clients ...

... collects information about ...

20

Project work

Create a survey about a topic from this unit or something you would like to know more about.

1 Decide if you want to collect facts or opinions and choose between a written survey and interview questions. The unit contains many examples.

2 Collect as many answers to your questions as you can and prepare to report on what you found out in class.

21 Pronunciation: stressing

Underline the word in each sentence which should be stressed to make the meaning clear.

1 Did you see the marketing manager yesterday? – No, I spoke to her on the phone.
2 Did you see the marketing manager yesterday? – No, I saw her on Tuesday.
3 Are Claudia and Rosa working on the project? – Yes, both of them are.
4 Everyone seems very busy at the moment. – Yes, even the boss has a lot to do!
5 Would you like me to organize a meeting? – It's OK, thanks, I can do it myself.
6 Would you like me to organize a meeting? – I think a conference call would be better.

22 Useful language

Which phrase is the odd one out in each set? Explain why by completing the explanations.

1 a Would that suit you? b Do you have any suggestions? c Could you make Tuesday?
(a) and ( ) are ways of *making arrangements*. ( ) is a way of *asking for help*.

2 a I know it's short notice, but ... b I was wondering if we could discuss a discount. c I see your point, but ...
( ) and ( ) are ways of ______. ( ) is a way of ______.

3 a Excuse me, did you say ...? b Am I right that you ...? c Could you put that into other words?
( ) and ( ) are ways of ______. ( ) is a way of ______.

4 a That's one way of putting it, but ... b Before I forget, ... c By the way, ...
( ) and ( ) are ways of ______. ( ) is a way of ______.

23 Listening: different pronunciations

A 40 Listen to what Helen, who works at the Shanghai office of Canada Wood, says about her job and answer the questions.

1 What is Helen's job?
2 What material does she work with?
3 What successes does she talk about?
4 What aspect of her work is sometimes frustrating?

B Listen again while reading the transcript on page 99. What features of her pronunciation do you notice? Do any of them make it difficult to understand her?

Before the next class Make a word cloud like the one on page 60 of about 8 – 10 words and expressions you use in your job. If you don't know the English terms, look them up.

For the next unit Find out how your company recruits new staff. Which channels are used? How easy is it to find information about job vacancies on your company's website?

08 Talent spotting

1

A The word cloud contains terms connected to Human Resources. Which of the terms **a** do you know and use, **b** do you understand, but not use yet and **c** are unknown?

professional development · staff · orientation · CV · staffing requirements · career fair · talent · head-hunter · intern · position · core skills · trainee · application · networking event · bonus · applicant · recruitment · candidate · incentives · promotion · career ladder · probationary period · interview · in-company training · employees · skills shortage · resume · vacancy · job · apprentice · staff turnover

B Answer the questions with words from **1A**.

1 Which terms refer to **a** a person or people and **b** a problem?
2 Find pairs of words with the same or similar meanings.
3 Which terms can be used in other contexts (not only in connection with recruitment)?
4 Find the terms which match these definitions:
   a The first three to six months in a new job before you get a permanent contract.
   b A better job in the same company.
   c Money or benefits which are given to staff to motivate them to work harder.

C What would you say to a friend who wants to get a better job? Use as many words from **1A** as you can.

2

A There are many words and expressions in English which include the word *job*. Complete the sentences with the most suitable expressions below. Then write your own sentences for the expressions you didn't use.

job application • job board • job centre • job description • job hunting • job satisfaction • job security • job sharing • job vacancies • on-the-job training

1 I wanted to work part-time after my daughter was born, so I decided to try ______ with one of my colleagues.
2 Outsourcing may have a negative impact on ______ for people in certain occupations.
3 A ______ is a website which lists ______. Employers pay for this service.
4 I want to have a responsible and worthwhile job, so ______ is my biggest priority.
5 I started ______ last year, but I still haven't found my dream job.

B Are there any common expressions in your own language with the word *job*?

*The word **job** is used in English for all kinds of work and occupations.*

3

Exchange the word cloud you created for your own job (Before the next class, page 61) with a partner. Which of the terms in your partner's cloud do you know and use, do you understand, but not use yet and are unknown? Teach each other any unknown words.

4

A Common ways of recruiting staff are offering internships, asking for employee referrals, recruiting internally, and advertising vacancies on job boards. Think about your own company (For the next unit, page 61) and add more strategies, if possible.

employee referral = recommendation from a member of staff

B Which of the ways mentioned in **4A** have you used? Which was the most successful for you? If you had to look for a new job now, which ones would you use?

5

Language focus: describing career paths

1 Read what Megan says about her career so far. Notice how she talks about each stage.

"After I *finished* my traineeship, I *worked* as an intern for six months in an Italian construction company. It *was* a great experience and *has had* an impact on my long-term career goals. At the moment, I'*m applying* for promotion so that I can work internationally. I'*ve been* with the company for two years now. I *got* my job here through a recommendation from a friend who *has been working* here for over five years now. At first I *worked* in her department, but then I *moved* to my present job in marketing. I *enjoy* it a lot, but I hope I get the promotion!"

2 Write the stages of Megan's career into the timeline below.

______ → ______ → ______ → ______ → ______

6

Tell your partner how you got your present job. How long have you been working for the company? Have you ever moved departments? What can you remember about the application process?

7

A 41 Oluchi works in the HR department of a multinational engineering company in Lagos, Nigeria. The company employs expats and local staff. Listen to what she says about their recruitment strategy and underline the verb forms you hear. Why does she use them?

1 So let me tell you what **happens / would happen** in my department if we **want / wanted** to recruit.
2 If **there's / there was** a vacancy in a particular section, the Project Manager or Head of Department **asks / would ask** his staff for suggestions.
3 If the Project Manager **has / had** no candidate, he **passes / would pass** on the job description to our department and we do the recruitment.
4 Internal recruitment has lots of advantages, so if we **get / got** applications from our staff, we **look / would look** at them very closely.

B Listen again and answer the questions.

1 How did Oluchi get her job?
2 Why are job adverts in newspapers or on job boards not the most effective way to get a job?
3 According to Oluchi, how important are connections if you are looking for a job? Do you agree with her?
4 When is internal recruitment an important channel?
5 At the beginning of her talk, Oluchi tells us that different types of employees get different contracts. What differences do you think there could be?

C Imagine there is a vacancy in your own department, which strategy would you choose to fill it? Explain your choice.

8

If you had a new intern in your department, how would you help him/her get to know the company and how it's organized? Choose one of the points on the checklist and decide what you would say.

Checklist for new employees:

- ▢ show him/her around
- ▢ explain how technical equipment works
- ▢ introduce him/her to colleagues
- ▢ explain the company organigram

9

Language focus: the language of mentoring

1 Most interns have a mentor who **a** explains what their job is, **b** gives them specific tasks to do, **c** checks their progress and **d** gives feedback on their work. Put these sentences into the correct category (a – d).

1 ▢ How useful did you find the Excel training session this morning?
2 ▢ Your main task is to support us in expanding our customer base.
3 ▢ Based on my observations, your excellent language skills are your greatest asset.
4 ▢ Please make appointments with these clients for me.

2 Intern or mentor? Who is most likely to say each sentence? Write **I** or **M** in the boxes.

1 ▢ Sometimes it's helpful to start the conversation with some small talk.
2 ▢ I'll see to it this afternoon.
3 ▢ Could you tell me which European countries I should focus on?
4 ▢ How far have you got with the preparations for the event in July?
5 ▢ OK, I'll keep that in mind in future.
6 ▢ I've made all the arrangements with the caterers. Shall I send you the details?
7 ▢ Make sure the documents are ready for the meeting with Mr Czaja on Wednesday.
8 ▢ The results of our international market research will help you find prospects*.

**a prospect = a potential customer*
good prospects = a positive outlook for the future

10

A 42 Morten is a Norwegian intern at a German company. His supervisor, Sabine Meyer, has asked him to come to her office. Listen and answer the questions.

1 Why has Sabine Meyer asked Morten to come to see her?
2 How does the conversation start?
3 Sabine gives Morten some positive feedback. What does she praise?
4 What change does she ask him to make?

B Listen again and decide on the function of each phrase.

Sabine:
1 How was your trip?
2 Let's take a look at how far you've got with the customer survey.
3 Based on my observations of your work so far, ...

Morten:
1 That's a very big celebration in Norway, you know.
2 Let me check.
3 That makes sense.

11 What advice would you give the young people mentioned in this article? Use the sentence beginnings to help you express your opinion.

Recruiting young people for STEM jobs

Companies all over the globe can't find enough staff with STEM* skills, but TV shows like the US comedy series *The Big Bang Theory* may change this. According to recent research, 48 % of young people say watching the show has awakened their interest in STEM subjects.

However, the research also shows that many young people don't want to study science and maths-based subjects because they think they are dull, boring and uninteresting. 53 % seem convinced that STEM subjects are harder than other subjects and not much fun either. According to the survey, only 19 % of girls said they would like a career in engineering compared with 51 % of boys. Over a third of the girls think STEM industries are male-dominated.

Many don't know what working in these fields involves and 67 % think that only people with very high IQs can do such jobs. What they don't realize is that STEM jobs can be a lot of fun, are very creative and inspiring – and offer great career opportunities.

Abridged from: www.independent.co.uk

***STEM Subjects**

S = science *T = technology*
E = engineering *M = mathematics*

1 If I were you, I'd ...
2 If I had the chance myself, I would ...
3 If you're not interested in STEM subjects, then you should ...
4 I think you should ...
5 If you think ...
6 I think you need ...

---

12 **A** Science centres have opened in many cities to show the general public how interesting and fun science can be. If you have visited one, talk about what you did and saw.

B 43 What background and skills do the technical staff at a science centre need? Listen to the HR manager from Techmania, the science centre in Pilsen, Czech Republic talking about hiring an edutainer. Do you think you could do this job? Why? Why not?

edutainer = educator + entertainer

Film 4 If you would like to find out how science centres like Techmania make science and technology interesting and fun, watch the film *Lighting the fire*.

Before you watch, turn to the video worksheet on page 112. The exercises will help you make the most of the film.

C What skills do staff need **a** in your company or **b** in your department?

13

A Read the statement and look at the picture. How do you usually behave in these situations?

"Historically, meeting strangers was potentially dangerous, so people developed different ways of dealing with this situation. Now, when we walk past strangers in the street, some people pretend they know you and others pretend you don't exist!"

B Talk about any experiences you have had with the situations in **13A**. Think of as many reasons as you can for each kind of behaviour. What are positive and negative interpretations of each type of behaviour?

The positive thing about a lively conversation is …

The downside is that …

C Do you think the differences in behaviour are more individual or more cultural?

14

What would you say in these situations? Choose one of the options or add your own response. Share your responses in class.

You are talking to a colleague about an upcoming conference.
- ☐ I'm very excited about the conference.
- ☐ I hope the conference is going to be interesting.

You are telling a colleague that you can't do him/her the big favour he asked for.
- ☐ I'd love to help, but the trade fair starts tomorrow. I'm really sorry.
- ☐ It might be difficult.

A colleague has done some very good work.
- ☐ You're amazing! You've done a brilliant job.
- ☐ (you say nothing)

15

A Is your communication style more emotional or more reserved? Look at the characteristics of each style and put a cross on the line to show where you see yourself. Then compare the results in class.

Emotional speak loudly, speak fast, talk a lot, use overstatement, use a lot of gestures, interrupt, have no silent phases, prefer speaking to writing

Reserved speak quietly, speak slowly, say only what is necessary, use understatement, use few gestures, take turns while speaking, have silent phases, communicate by writing and speaking

emotional ←——————————————————————→ **reserved**

B In groups of four, role-play a meeting at an international conference.

Partner A → **File 42**, page 70. **Partner B** → **File 43**, page 74.
Partner C → **File 44**, page 80. **Partner D** → **File 45**, page 85.

C Answer these questions individually before you share your responses with your group and then in class. How similar are your answers?

1 How easy was it to play your role?
2 What impression do you think you made on the others?
3 What impression did each of the others make on you?

16

A How do you talk about your own abilities and successes (at work or in your private life)? Do you talk about them at all? Do you compliment others on their achievements?

I'm an expert on …

I know a little bit about …

My team always comes to me if there's a problem.

I've learned quite a lot about the software, but only because I knew so little before.

B Rate these statements for yourself (1 = agree totally … 6 = disagree totally). Then compare your answers in class.

1 I enjoy speaking openly about my achievements.	1 2 3 4 5 6
2 I enjoy getting compliments and respond openly.	1 2 3 4 5 6
3 My own achievements are more important to me than the achievements of my team or my company.	1 2 3 4 5 6
4 I like complimenting others on their achievements.	1 2 3 4 5 6

C 44 Now listen to George and Jack talking at a networking event during a conference. How does each one talk about his achievements and compliment the other?

MBA = Master of Business Administration

17

Language focus: talking about skills and achievements

1 When you have a job interview or an interview for promotion, it's a good idea to prepare to talk about what you can offer the employer. Which of the questions **a** refer to the past and which are **b** general statements with no reference to a time?

1 Looking back at your career so far, what have you done that …
- a ☐ … *had* a positive impact on your company?
- b ☐ … you *were* very proud of?
- c ☐ … you *enjoyed* doing?
- d ☐ … *was* a big challenge?

2 What do other people …
- a ☐ … *say* you're good at?
- b ☐ … often *ask* you to do?

3 When you work with others, …
- a ☐ … what role *do you prefer* in a team?
- b ☐ … how *do you solve* problems?

2 Choose at least two of the questions and answer them as if you were in an interview.
For example: In general, I *prefer* to make the decisions myself.
My former boss *said* I was very good at time management.

18

You can present your achievements positively by using a variety of strategies. Look at the examples and replace the underlined parts of the sentences with something you could say about your own skills and achievements.

1 **describing your strengths**: One of my strengths is that <u>I learn new things very quickly</u>.
2 **showing commitment**: In my last project, <u>we were under a lot of time pressure</u>, so <u>I worked overtime whenever it was needed</u>.
3 **claiming responsibility for success**: My <u>good relationship to our Chinese partners</u> led to a <u>very big increase in sales</u>.
4 **overcoming problems**: When we had a conflict <u>in our team, I organized a team day to clear the air</u>.

19

What are the advantages and disadvantages of internal recruitment? Is it a better option than recruiting externally? Discuss these questions with a partner or in small groups. Consider the issues below and any other ideas you have.

company culture • education • efficiency • experience • insider knowledge • loyalty • motivation • networks • new ideas • salary • speed • training costs

20

Language focus: reporting the results of a discussion

Use these sentence beginnings to report on your discussion in **19**.

We talked about ...

We said that ...

On the whole, we agreed that ...

We weren't sure how important ...

We didn't agree on one point. X said ... but the others ...

We came to the conclusion that ...

Think of a conversation you had at work recently and tell a partner what you talked about.

21

A Match these sentence halves to make a list of typical job interview questions.

1 Why don't you start by telling	A to leave your current job?
2 Tell me about a difficult situation you faced at work	B for this vacancy?
3 Why do you want	C me something about yourself?
4 What would you do	D about your current job?
5 Why did you apply	E during your first 90 days in the job?
6 What do you like	F and how you dealt with it.

B Competency-based interviews have become popular because employers think they show whether a candidate would perform well in the position. Choose one of the options below and note down how you would answer.

Tell me about a time when you ...

1 ... led or worked in a team which achieved its goal.
2 ... developed a creative solution to a problem.
3 ... helped people to work together.
4 ... were very satisfied with your own achievements.

C In an internal interview, the interviewer may ask some additional questions. Work with a partner and role-play the interview according to the instructions.

Partner A → **File 46**, page 74. **Partner B** → **File 47**, page 79.

D Now look at the interviewee's answers in **File 47** again and discuss other possible answers to the questions. Make up any details.

22

Project work

It has become common for interviewers to switch to English during a job interview.

1 If there was a job vacancy in your department and you were the interviewer, what would you want to know about the candidates? What questions would you ask in English?
2 In your group, pool all your questions and discuss and make a note of good answers.
3 Share your results with other groups.
4 Create an interview role-play to demonstrate how to make a good impression.
5 Make a list of questions and answers for your next job interview.

23 Vocabulary: words with two meanings

Complete each pair of sentences with the same word.

1 a I changed my job because I had no chance of __________ in my old company.
  b The company is offering a special __________ to try to win back customers.
2 a During the trade fair, there were no __________ at hotels near the fair grounds.
  b We advertise all our __________ on the job board.
3 a I'm disappointed to hear that the __________ at head office has already been filled.
  b If I were you, I'd change the __________ of your desk so you have more light.

24 Useful language

Mark the stages in your career along this timeline. Include events and achievements.

25 Grammar: 1st and 2nd conditional

Complete the sentences in a way which is true for you and share them with a partner. Choose one of the topics to talk about in more detail.

1 If I took a day off next week, I ...
2 If I get promotion, I ...
3 If I have time this evening, I ...
4 If I really want to impress a client, I ...
5 If my boss asked me to entertain a foreign business visitor, I ...
6 If there were fewer meetings, we ...

26 Listening: communication styles

45 Now listen to Morten talking about his internship at the German company and the differences he has noticed in communication styles. What does he say about these topics?

1 orientation for interns
2 interaction between colleagues
3 communication between himself and his supervisor
4 hierarchy

Looking back Look back through the book and find listening exercises in which people speak with accents you often come across in your own work. Refer to the *Listening to accents* worksheets on the **Simply Business** website for ideas on how to improve your listening skills.

Looking forward If there's an accent you need to become familiar with, you can find plenty of examples on the internet. The TED talks site is a good place to start.

APPENDIX Files

File 42

Unit 8 Exercise 15

You are at an international conference and are having lunch with three other participants. You are talking about a presentation you all attended. Read about your communication style and think for a few minutes about what you are going to say. Make up any details you like, but stick to your role.

- You were very impressed with the presentation and tell your partners about this in a loud voice.
- You thought the speaker was entertaining and she was well informed.
- Use a lot of gestures to emphasize your words.
- If someone disagrees with you, try to convince him/her of your opinion.

File 1

Unit 1 Exercise 7

Business card etiquette

Although there are some general rules for dealing with business cards in each country, you may see people behaving in different ways within one country.
In the UK and in North America, there are no special rituals or times when people exchange business cards. They are simply a networking tool and a quick way of giving your contact details to someone who is interested in your products or services.
In Italy, too, business cards can be exchanged at any time during a meeting. If someone crosses out their academic or professional titles when they give you their card, this shows that a closer relationship has developed and that you don't need to use formal titles when addressing your Italian partner.
In Scandinavia, people usually exchange cards after some small talk.
When you arrive for an appointment in Spain or Turkey, it's a good idea to give your business card to the receptionist.
In Germany, people don't hand out so many cards. Here the person is giving you permission to contact them, and you should treat business cards as confidential, private property.
Although people tend to hand out business cards very freely in the US, you should wait for someone to ask for your card. If that doesn't happen, ask the other person for their card.
In some parts of the world it is very rude to write on a business card, but this is acceptable in the US. You could write the answer to a question you asked on the back of a business card, for example.

File 3

Unit 1 Exercise 13

MAKING THE MOST OF A TRADE FAIR

Well-trained staff can mean the difference between a trade fair which is successful and one which is a waste of time and money. It's not enough to hand out company literature and business cards to staff. Make sure they can explain what the company does in a few sentences. Provide printed product overviews of the features, prices, product reviews, etc. for each potential target group to make it easier for staff to know what to focus on.

Staff also need pre-show client profiles with the names of any VIP clients and information on what action to take if they visit the booth. Provide a list of the frequently asked questions they can expect to hear.

Before the show, take staff on a virtual tour of the exhibition halls, so that they can locate the registration desk, event and demonstration areas, the storage and meeting rooms, the press room, etc.

File 7

Unit 2 Exercise 14

You are the caller. This is your first phone conversation with a supplier who has worked with your company for a few years. In future you are going to be the contact person. You are phoning to make an appointment for your boss to visit the supplier's factory.

- Before you start, make up the details: the name of your boss, when he/she wants to visit the supplier, the reason for the visit, etc.
- ask if it's a good time to call
- the name of the supplier is difficult to pronounce
- you don't want to waste time on small talk
- the supplier has a strong accent which you don't understand very well
- the telephone connection is not very good

File 9

Unit 3 Exercise 2

1 Ask your partner which countries the letters in BRICS and CAPPT stand for. Use these expressions to help you.

BRICS Brazil, Russia, India, China, South Africa
CAPPT Chile, Argentina, Peru, The Philippines, Thailand

*Do you know what the **B** in BRICS stands for?*

*Can you guess what the **C** in CAPPT stands for? It's not the same as the **C** in BRICS.*

*I'll give you a hint. **T** is a country in Asia.*

Do you need some help? It's a country in South America.

That's a good guess, but in fact it's …

2 Now answer your partner's questions. Use these expressions to help you.

***M** must be …, but I don't know the other letters.*

*I'm sure that **N** stands for …*

*This is a guess, but **T** might be …*

*I've no idea what **V** stands for, but **I** might be …*

Can you give me a hint?

File 11

Unit 3 Exercise 5

Winter time / Summer time

In many countries, clocks are put forward in the summer and back in the winter. The date for putting clocks back is not the same in all countries and varies from September to November. The date for putting clocks forward can be in March or April. Another name for summer time is Daylight Saving Time (DST).

Holiday periods

There are certain times of the year when the normal work routine is interrupted and when it can be difficult to get things done. These periods differ quite a lot from country to country. In Europe, work slows down for a couple of weeks around Christmas and New Year, but in South America this period lasts longer because the summer holidays are in January and February. Especially in Brazil, things get back to normal only after Carnival.
It may be difficult to reach colleagues in Finland between the midsummer festival in June and the end of July as this is when many people go off to their summer houses to relax. The school summer holidays are very long.
During Ramadan, which has different dates every year, it is often business as usual. In fact, employees often start work earlier than usual because they get up before the sun rises to eat breakfast and then just go to work after that. However, many people are on holiday for a week or two to celebrate the end of Ramadan.
Chinese employees usually take a holiday of a week or ten days for the Chinese New Year in January or February and for the National Day holiday from the beginning of October.

File 13

Unit 3 Exercise 9

Complete the diary page with typical activities you do at work. Use the ideas you had in **7C** (page 24) to help you. Then role-play the two situations.

Tomorrow's date: ____________

Time	Activity

Situation 1

Something unexpected has happened, so you can't do some of the things you were planning to do tomorrow. Ask your partner for help.

Situation 2

Your partner asks you for help. Refuse at least one of his/her requests and explain why.

File 16

Unit 3 Exercise 14

"Chemi is part of a major Italian pharmaceuticals group based in Milan. I work near Rome at the facility which focuses on API production for the pharmaceutical industry. API stands for Active Pharmaceutical Ingredient. The API is the most important substance in a tablet or other medicine. We export about 90% of our products to markets in other European countries, Asia and North America.
For several reasons, most Italian companies working in this field have moved their production to Eastern Europe, Asia or Latin America. The reasons could be to reduce costs or to be closer to certain raw materials. Sometimes this is also done to be able to produce APIs which are covered by patents in Europe. This was one reason why we expanded to Brazil and set up a subsidiary there. Another reason was that we wanted to increase our production capacity in general."

File 18

Unit 3 Exercise 25

Take turns to read out your clues to your partner. Wait until he/she guesses the word, then you both write it down. If your partner can't guess, give some help. All the words are in **1A** on page 22.

Clues

1 To sell goods abroad. (export)
3 To put parts and components together. (assemble)
5 To buy and sell. (trade)
7 To find new staff. (recruit)

File 22

Unit 4 Exercise 12

Role-play 1

You work for Piacentini Costruzione. This is your first meeting with a member of the local government of a seaside town on the Mediterranean Sea. They are against the building of a harbour although the national government is interested. Give advice based on the success of a similar project in Libya.

File 23

Unit 4 Exercise 12

Role-play 2

You are the CEO of a plant for agricultural waste water treatment. You are interested in WeDoTech's biofiltration methods. At first you are sceptical, but finally accept that changing to their technology would be a good idea.

File 29

Unit 5 Exercise 5

Ukraine

Companies wanting to outsource to unknown offshore or nearshore partners face several challenges. One of them is choosing the right country.

Nearshoring has many advantages over offshoring. It's quicker and easier to get to your nearshore partner if a face-to-face meeting becomes necessary. Travel costs are lower than to locations far away, and time differences are very small, so it's never difficult to reach someone. This is especially important if we need to solve an urgent problem quickly.

EU nationals can enter Ukraine without a visa, and the way of working is the same as in the rest of Europe. Companies here can offer very competitive prices as salaries, taxes and infrastructure costs are much lower than in the rest of Europe. However, although salaries are low, the workforce, especially in the fields of science and technology, are well educated. For example, Ukraine is one of the top ten countries worldwide with the most highly-skilled and certified IT specialists. There are a large number of outsourcing providers for small and medium-sized businesses. In addition, it is easy to find staff with foreign language skills. Many people speak English, and it is not difficult to find speakers of German, French or Spanish. Everyone also speaks Russian.

File 31

Unit 6 Exercise 8

Dialogue 1

To ask the question like this would be quite normal and not impolite in Singapore. Our priority is quick efficient communication, so people don't worry about using full sentences.

Dialogue 3

In the whole of Ireland (the Republic and Northern Ireland) it's common to use negative sentences to be polite. For example, instead of saying "Could you ..." one would say something like, "You couldn't have a look at this for a wee minute, could you?" This shows understanding for the other person by saying "I know you don't have time for this, but ... ." By adding "a minute" we want to emphasize that we don't want to take up too much of the other's time.

File 37

Unit 7 Exercise 6

Why activity-based working is the best solution:

- fewer desks = less office space = lower costs for the company
- flexible working = better work-life balance
- better work-life balance = more job satisfaction = fewer sick days
- no fixed workspace = more communication and collaboration as team members move around the workspace
- flexible workspaces = increase in creativity = increased productivity
- choice of workspace = good for individual and team work
- quiet work areas = better concentration = higher quality of work and speed of getting things done
- flexible workplace = motivated staff
- attractive to new staff = good for recruitment
- flexible workplaces = easier to react to changes in the way we work

File 40

Unit 7 Exercise 17

Situation 1

Tell your partner about a difficult situation you had to deal with recently. If you can't think of one, make one up. Use the list of expressions below to check that your partner understands you. Respond to any questions he/she asks you.

- Do you have any questions before I go on?
- Maybe I haven't explained that very well.
- Am I speaking too quickly?
- My English isn't very fluent, so maybe I should ...

Situation 2

You partner is going to tell you about a difficult situation he/she had to deal with recently. You don't understand him/her very well, so clarify and confirm what you hear. Read through the list of expressions below before you start. Cross out the ones you use.

- That's interesting. What happened then?
- Excuse me, did you say ...?
- Just to check if I understand you correctly, ...
- What was that word again?
- Am I right that you ...?
- Yes, I see what you mean.
- That sounds difficult!
- Ah, so you mean ...?
- Can/Could you put that in other words?
- I know what you mean, but ...
- I don't (quite) understand what you mean by ...
- Let me put it in another way ...

File 43

Unit 8 Exercise 15

You are at an international conference and are having lunch with three other participants. You are talking about a presentation you all attended. Read about your communication style and think for a few minutes about what you are going to say. Make up any details you like, but stick to your role.

- You liked the presentation and explain to your partners in a lot of detail what you liked about it. (e.g. the presenter obviously knew the subject, she answered difficult questions very well, gave a lot of important background information about the project, etc.)
- Speak slowly and clearly.
- You're interested in knowing what the others thought of the presentation, so encourage everyone to speak.
- You never interrupt other people when they're talking.

File 46

Unit 8 Exercise 21

You are the interviewer. Your department has a job vacancy, and a colleague from a different department in your company has applied for the job. Think of some general questions to create a positive atmosphere at the beginning of the interview, then ask the questions below in any order you like. Don't ask the questions as if you have already decided not to give him/her the job!

1 What will you do if you don't get this job?
2 Does your manager know that you have applied for this job?
3 What do you know about our department?
4 Have you ever had a conflict with anyone in your department? How did you deal with it?
5 Why have you applied for another position in our company?

File 2

Unit 1 Exercise 7

Business card etiquette

Although there are some general rules for dealing with business cards in each country, you may see people behaving in different ways within one country.

In western countries, it is quite normal to keep business cards in a wallet or just in a pocket, and there are usually no rules about exactly when to offer a card. This is different in Asia, where the exchange of business cards is a formal introduction at the first meeting. People treat cards with a lot of respect, and there are fixed protocols for their exchange.

Generally, as a visitor, you should offer your card first. Before the meeting, take the number of cards you will need to exchange out of your business card holder (you must have one – it is rude to keep them in a pocket or wallet) so that you have them ready. You should introduce yourself when you offer your card. Be sure to mention your company and your name. Also remember to give and receive cards with both hands. When you receive the other person's card, it is polite to confirm their name, say thank you and make a comment about the company, its location or its business. Always remember that the highest ranking people exchange cards first.

Don't put the cards away immediately – keep them on the table during the meeting and look at them from time to time. It is a good way to learn the names. In China or Japan, you should never write anything on a business card.

In many countries, such as India or in the Middle East, for example, it is extremely impolite to use your left hand to hand out your business cards.

File 4

Unit 1 Exercise 13

Making the most of a trade fair

The impression your company makes on a visitor in the first four seconds is extremely important, so train staff to stand at the front of the booth and start conversations. Tell them to smile, make eye-contact with visitors and look relaxed – not as if they are guarding the booth!

Train your staff in good booth behaviour: no eating in the booth, no checking emails in the booth, no working on reports, no talking on cell phones. If visitors see this, they will walk away. Make sure staff can introduce themselves and answer a few questions about their work.

Discuss the show schedule and give each person a specific role, such as coordinating relations with the press, being responsible for technical issues or tidying up the booth during the day.

File 8

Unit 2 Exercise 14

You receive a phone call from a new member of staff at a company you have worked with for a few years. You are one of their suppliers.

- you are busy, but the customer is very important to you
- try to create a friendly relationship with the caller because he/she will be the company contact person in future
- the caller speaks very quickly, so you don't understand everything he/she says
- the first date the caller suggests for a visit isn't possible
- the telephone connection is not very good
- summarize what you have understood

File 10

Unit 3 Exercise 2

1 Answer your partner's questions. Use these expressions to help you.

__R__ must be …, but I don't know the other letters.

I'm sure that __C__ stands for …

I've no idea what __A__ stands for, but it might be …

Can you give me a hint?

This is a guess, but one of the __P__s might be …

2 Ask your partner which countries the letters in MINT and CIVITS stand for. Use these expressions to help you.

MINT Mexico, Indonesia, Nigeria, Turkey
CIVETS Colombia, Indonesia, Vietnam, Egypt, Turkey, South Africa

Do you know what the __M__ in MINT stands for?

Can you guess what the __C__ in CIVETS stands for? It's not the same as in BRICS.

I'll give you a hint. __V__ is a country in Asia.

Do you need some help? Two of the countries are in Africa.

That's a good guess, but in fact it's …

File 12

Unit 3 Exercise 5

Time zones

There are 24 standard time zones in the world, each one an hour apart. In India, Iran and Venezuela the difference to the previous time zone is only half an hour. Although, China covers four time zones geographically, Beijing time is standard all over the country. This is not the case in other big countries like the US, Canada, Russia and Brazil.

In June, when it is 23:50 in Auckland, this is the time in other places around the world:

04:50 Vancouver	06:50 Mexico City	08:50 Rio de Janeiro	13:50 Amsterdam	14:50 Ankara
17:20 Mumbai	18:50 Jakarta	19:50 Singapore	20:50 Tokyo	21:50 Sydney

The working week

In most places (Europe, US, China, Turkey, etc.), the working week is from Monday to Friday, but there are quite a few exceptions:

Sunday – Thursday → in Dubai, Israel and Saudi Arabia
Monday – Saturday → in Kenya, Indonesia, India and New Zealand
Saturday – Thursday → in Iran

In countries with a six-day working week, the sixth day is usually only a half-day. People may not work six days a week in all sectors.

File 14

Unit 3 Exercise 9

Complete the diary page with typical activities you do at work. Use the ideas you had in **7C** (page 24) to help you. Then role-play the two situations.

The day after tomorrow's date: ____________________

Time	Activity

Situation 1
Your partner asks you for help. Refuse at least one of his/her requests and explain why.

Situation 2
Something unexpected has happened, so you can't do some of the things you were planning to do the day after tomorrow. Ask your partner for help.

File 17

Unit 3 Exercise 14

"WiSMa is a German company with its headquarters in Freiburg. It's a subsidiary of the university hospital there. The company provides a wide range of services and materials for companies and organizations in the healthcare industry, from sourcing medical equipment, to managing the supply chain or from organizing medical conferences to managing catering services. WiSMa started working internationally as a way to expand its business and increase revenue.
I'm the head of WiSMa's China office in Beijing. In China, we are the exclusive agents of a number of German and British manufacturers of medical equipment and already have a large network of partners and distributors here. In addition, our main activities in China are organizing conferences, carrying out market research and purchasing support services for European companies who need that to do business in China."

File 19

Unit 3 Exercise 25

Take turns to read out your clues to your partner. Wait until he/she guesses the word, then you both write it down. If your partner can't guess, give some help. All the words are in **1 A** on page 22.

Clues

2 To give someone goods or services in exchange for money. (sell)
4 To take control of another company. (take over)
6 To find and then buy the materials you need for your business. (source)
8 Another word for buy. (purchase)

File 24

Unit 4 Exercise 12

Role-play 1

You are a representative of the local government of a seaside town on the Mediterranean Sea. The national government plans to build a harbour in your town, but you are not happy about this. You do not want to accept the advice from the representative of Piacentini Costruzione.

File 25

Unit 4 Exercise 12

Role-play 2

You work for WeDoTech. This is the first meeting with the CEO of an agricultural waste water plant. He/She is interested in your biofiltration methods. Explain why your methods are better than traditional ones.

File 30

Unit 5 Exercise 5

Vietnam

There's no question that most offshored work is done in India or China. However, Vietnam is also becoming a popular outsourcing location, especially for information technology companies.

One reason why Ho Chi Minh City is among the top five outsourcing cities in the world is that production costs there are very low. Salaries are 40% lower than in India and China, for example. Taxes and the cost of property rates are similar to other Asian countries. In addition, the Vietnamese government offers great incentives to promote more foreign investment.

However, it's not only a question of cost. Vietnam is often chosen as an offshore location because the young generation of workers there is highly motivated and has excellent technological skills. Every year more than 25,000 technical engineers graduate from universities in Vietnam. They are extremely flexible and willing to work very long hours to finish projects on time. They are always punctual and like working in teams. Overall, staff in Vietnam are very loyal to their companies, so the turnover rate is low, much lower than in many other countries like India and China.

IT staff can communicate well in English, especially in writing. To improve the standard of English skills, many outsourcing companies offer language courses and use English as the working language in the office.

File 32

Unit 6 Exercise 8

Dialogue 2

In Singapore and in China, people tend to be very direct when they speak English. This is especially true when speaking to people they know well. So what sounds very abrupt and rude to others is quite OK and polite. In many cases, they speak like this because they are translating directly from Chinese.

Dialogue 4

In Germany, it's very common to hear people answer a question in this way. It's not rude, it's just a direct answer. Many Germans think that "of course" is just another way of saying yes.

File 38

Unit 7 Exercise 6

Why activity-based working is not a solution:

- people like routine and structure = change makes people afraid
- decisions to be taken every day (where to work, where to store equipment, etc.) = waste of time
- more time has to be spent on organizing work = less time for working
- own desk and office = part of own identity
- no desk = loss of status
- clean-desk policy = not convenient
- redesigning the workspace and increased need for technology = high costs at the beginning
- difficult to implement many ideas because of regulations on fire safety, lighting, heating, ventilation, amount of space per employee, standards and norms for furniture, IT equipment, etc.
- staff work outside office = lack of control by managers

File 41

Unit 7 Exercise 17

Situation 1

Your partner is going to tell you about a difficult situation he/she had to deal with recently. You don't understand him/her very well, so clarify and confirm what you hear. Read through the list of expressions before you start. Cross out the ones you use.

- And that means ...?
- I thought we were talking about ...?
- Can/ Could you start again right from the beginning?
- Eh?
- I still don't get it.
- It's going in one ear and out the other.
- I'm sorry, but I have no idea what you mean.
- I've never heard the word ... before.
- I'm totally confused.
- Sorry?
- You've lost me now.
- I don't know what you mean.

Situation 2

Tell your partner about a difficult situation you had to deal with recently. If you can't think of one, make one up. Use the list of expressions below to check that your partner understands you. Respond to any questions he/she asks you.

- Do you have any questions before I go on?
- Maybe I haven't explained that very well.
- Am I speaking too quickly?
- My English isn't very fluent, so maybe I should ...

File 47

Unit 8 Exercise 21

You are the interviewee. You have applied for a job in a different department of your company. Before the interview starts, read through the answers you are going to give and think about what the questions might be. The interviewer may start with some general questions to create a positive atmosphere. Then he/she will ask you five internal interview questions. Choose the most suitable answer to each one.

1. At our last company networking event, I had a long conversation with two members of your team so that gave me some insight into the work of the department.
2. There have been disagreements, but nothing major. I think that it's important to understand the other person's point of view, so I take the time to do this and work out a solution together.
3. I'll be disappointed as I think I have the skills to do the job well, but I'll still have a position I enjoy.
4. Yes, I've discussed my application with my manager so that she understands my reasons for taking this step.
5. I'm very motivated by challenges, and I think this position will give me the chance to use my skills and experience effectively in an environment I know well.

File 44

Unit 8 Exercise 15

You are at an international conference and are having lunch with three other participants. You are talking about a presentation you all attended. Read about your communication style and think for a few minutes about what you are going to say. Make up any details you like, but stick to your role.

- You didn't like the presentation very much and want to explain exactly why not.
- You found the presenter entertaining but thought that she didn't have anything new to say.
- You don't think that the project results she talked about are convincing.
- You speak very quickly and can't wait for other people to finish what they are saying, especially if you don't agree with them, but you would still like to hear everyone's opinion.

File 5

Unit 1 Exercise 15

How would you react if someone said the following to you at a trade fair? Choose the two responses you think are most suitable for each one.

A ☐ ☐ You should talk to Beatrix Barreira about that. I'll ask her to contact you as soon as possible.
B ☐ ☐ Please sit down for a moment. Exhibitions are very tiring, aren't they?
C ☐ ☐ I'll get back to you with more information by the beginning of next week.
D ☐ ☐ Shall I get you something to drink? Tea or coffee?

1 Yes, they are. I'd love to relax for a moment.
2 Shall I come back later to talk to her?
3 Thanks, I wouldn't say no to a coffee.
4 That's a bit late, I'm afraid. Is there anyone else I can speak to?
5 You're right, but I have an appointment in five minutes so I'll have to go.
6 OK. Thanks for your help.
7 Thanks very much, but I've just had a cup.
8 OK. I'll give you my card so that she can call me.

File 6

Unit 1 Exercise 23

Six tips for making the most of a conference with social media

1. Choose a hashtag for your conference that speakers and attendees can use to talk about their experience. This allows people who are not at the conference to follow the conversation.
2. The best conference hashtags are short, easy to remember, and include the name of your company or the conference.
3. Invite attendees to contact you via social media channels like Facebook and LinkedIn. Use the services to invite visitors to your booth for a surprise gift, to remind visitors of events, and to present your products. Only about 20% of the content should be directly promotional.
4. Monitor conversations during the conference and respond. Encourage attendees to have virtual conversations with other attendees via Twitter or Instagram.
5. Pick one or two channels (the ones your customers use most) and focus on them.
6. Visual materials create maximum impact, so use photos and video when it makes sense.

What's the ideal length?

Opinions differ, but here are some recommendations. Remember that every message should be as long as necessary to present the message – but no longer.

Tweet: 70 – 100 characters
Facebook post: 40 characters
Instagram caption: 130 characters
Instagram video: 10 seconds
Email subject line: 28 – 36 characters
Hashtag: max. 6 characters

File 15

Unit 3 Exercise 10

1 Cheap is a more negative word and may suggest low quality. Inexpensive sounds as if it is a good buy.

2 In Europe (except UK/Ireland) "that's interesting" can be a positive comment and mean what it says. In English-speaking countries, it can also be used to show disagreement or that you are not interested. In Asia, it can be a way of saying no.

3 In many places, compromise is seen as a positive outcome. In China, it has the negative association of giving up the best solution under pressure.

4 Lunch can be a sandwich (Belgium, Netherlands) or the main meal of the day (Germany, Eastern Europe). Lunch can take 30 minutes (China) or 60 – 90 minutes (France).

A bicycle can be a modern way of travelling for people who care about the environment (Netherlands, Denmark, Germany) or something only used by poor people who cannot afford a car (China and many other parts of Asia). It can be an alternative to a car or just transport for leisure activities.

In many parts of the world, most people never have a holiday and when they do, it is a time to visit family. For other people, a holiday can mean a time to relax on the beach (Europe) or to visit faraway places (Europe, Japan, richer people in Asia).

File 20

Unit 4 Exercise 5

Expression	Meaning
You can say that again.	I completely agree.
You see?	Do you understand?
The meal was sort of expensive.	It was a bit too expensive.
See you later.	In US English: See you again sometime.
Take it easy.	Relax, don't worry/get angry.
Let's keep in touch.	Let's stay in contact with each other.
Oh, come on!	I don't believe you
Never mind.	It doesn't matter.
It's up to you.	You can/should make a decision.
Thank goodness for that.	What a relief!

File 21

Unit 4 Exercise 6

The meaning of all four sayings is "I'm very busy".

	Language	Idiom	Meaning
1	Portuguese/Brazilian Portuguese	*Não ter mãos a medir*	My hands are too full.
2	German	*Land unter*	I'm flooded with work.
3	English	I'm up to my eyes in work. / I'm up to ears in work.	
4	Chinese	焦头烂额 *(jiāo tóu làn é)*	My head is burning and my forehead is smashed.

File 26

Unit 4 Exercise 17

Greeting the audience:	Nice to see you all today.
Introducing the topic:	We're going to talk about ... today.
Explaining the structure:	Let me give you an overview of ...
Starting the presentation:	So the first issue is ...
Moving on to the next point:	Now, let me move on.
Referring back or forward:	If you remember, I ...
Clarifying a point:	What I mean is ...
Concluding:	So, in conclusion, ...
Thanking the audience:	Thanks for your interest.
Asking for questions:	Does anyone have a question?

File 27

Unit 4 Exercise 20

Brazil

When you give a presentation in Brazil, it's a good idea to:

- be enthusiastic about the topic and talk directly to the audience
- take time to introduce yourself and your company and explain the background to your topic
- show your interest in cooperation with Brazilians
- engage with the audience on a personal level
- be creative if you want to keep the audience's attention
- be prepared for lots of questions
- dress very professionally – looking good is important!

China

When you give a presentation in China, it's a good idea to:

- show respect to your audience
- dress professionally, but simply
- be humorous, but be sure your humour will be understood
- talk about the history and reputation of your company and your position
- present a clear and detailed outline of your talk, explain the background
- leave technical details until later
- promise to provide advice and support
- be very explicit, plenty of text and graphics on slides
- expect people to ask their questions during a private conversation

France

When you give a presentation in France, it's a good idea to:

- be honest with your information and not to exaggerate
- take time to present background information
- be enthusiastic, but not over-enthusiastic
- speak as freely as possible to show you know the topic well
- leave the main point until the end
- avoid having too much text on a slide
- be friendly but a bit formal

India

When you give a presentation in India, it's a good idea to:
- show that you are competent by speaking freely
- engage with the audience on a personal level
- communicate in a lively way
- present the background and make sure you don't overload your slides with text
- remember that the big picture is more important than too many technical details
- tell a story, but reach a balance between enthusiasm and calm
- show flexibility

Italy

When you give a presentation in Italy, it's a good idea to:
- realize that formal business presentations are not so common
- be prepared for a more informal presentation to a smaller audience
- show you know what you're talking about
- interact a lot with the audience because Italian audiences prefer a discussion
- have a flexible structure, so you can react to the audience
- give practical examples
- dress very professionally because it's important to look good

Russia

When you give a presentation in Russia, it's a good idea to:
- start by being reserved and not to smile unless you have a reason
- avoid making your topic sound too simple by being specific
- give a detailed introduction to the topic and the background
- give a lot of detailed information on how things work
- have lots of text and visual input on your slides
- position your company compared to competitors
- show you understand the local market

UAE

When you give a presentation in the UAE, it's a good idea to:
- mention positive impressions of the country
- use colourful language, tell stories to get your point across, show emotions, exaggerate
- show that you know your topic well
- avoid including too many facts and figures (put them in a handout)
- explain why your topic is relevant for the audience
- repeat your main points
- remember that the product from a company with an excellent reputation is more important than the price

USA

When you give a presentation in the USA, it's a good idea to:
- start with some small talk to create an informal atmosphere
- get to the point of the talk quickly
- attract the attention of the audience with an interesting story or a surprising fact
- show the impact of your product and focus on results – the background is not so important
- be enthusiastic but not to exaggerate
- create clear and simple slides without too much text
- summarize your talk and explain the next steps
- expect questions during the talk

File 28

Unit 4 Exercise 21

The emergency kit

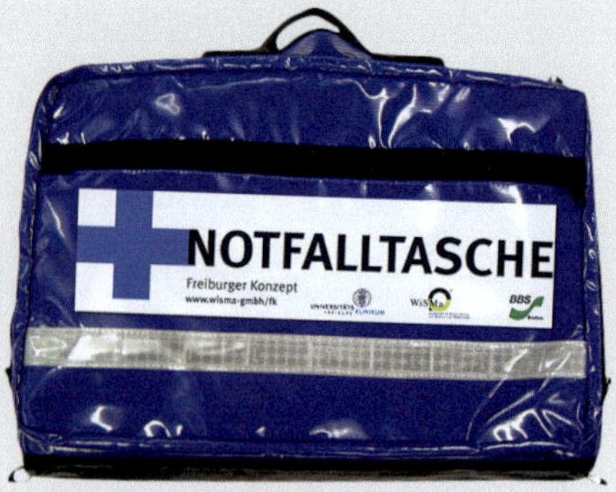

- The kit was developed by professionals from emergency medicine and the local association for disabled athletes.
- It provides equipment for treating sports-related medical emergencies. This varies from dealing with heart problems to broken bones, wounds and muscle problems.
- The kit's design combines both durability and mobility for on-the-go purposes.
- The kits are convenient, lifelong products for sports clubs and athletes.
- The kit's modular structure is its unique characteristic. The modules are colour coded and easy to recognize to avoid wasting any time when dealing with an emergency. Each customer chooses their own combination of modules.
- Each component of the kit was assessed for its cost effectiveness.
- The kits are assembled with high quality components at good prices for the end-users.
- The inspection management service saves time and money because the serial number and inspection interval for each medical device in the kit are kept in a central database. This provides maintenance transparency, and the customer is informed when the device is due for its next inspection.
- The service also provides an up-to-date inspection certificate and saves the customer time from having to track this information.
- The customer is informed when devices or individual components of devices have passed their expiry date and need to be replaced. All components and devices are in stock.

File 33

Unit 6 Exercise 9

Marco's German friends told him that internet access is not always available to customers in German cafés and restaurants, so this wasn't an unusual situation. The waitress just wanted to tell him directly that it wasn't possible and didn't intend to be rude. They also said it might have been a good idea to order something before asking for the access code.

In many Asian countries, it is the norm for customers to have internet access in cafés, etc. However, in a similar case, Chih-Wei said a waitress in Taiwan would probably have said something like, "I'm sorry, but we don't have internet here."

File 34

Unit 6 Exercise 13

This happened after I just started my very first job. I was working as an IT consultant with some colleagues from India at one of our client's sites in Padang. I wanted them to taste one of the local specialities there, so I recommended they tried *rendang*. This is a tasty beef dish. I ordered it for myself, but they chose something else. While I was eating, I told them how good it tasted, but they didn't seem interested.
Liya, Indonesia

We arranged an evening reception for our Kuwaiti customers and provided a magnificent buffet meal. We thought this was a good idea because everyone could eat the food they preferred. We made sure that all the food was halal and told them this. All the dishes were labelled in English. The CEO of our company made a welcoming speech, and then I took them over to the buffet and invited them to help themselves. I had to take an important phone call and I was really surprised when I went back to the table because our guests had already left. I don't think they ate any of the delicious food.
Valentina, Italy

File 35

Unit 6 Exercise 14

1 A *rambutan* is similar to a lychee, but a bit bigger and with a hairy skin.
2 *Boorsoq* is a kind of Mongolian doughnut. It's often eaten as a dessert with sugar, butter or honey.
3 *Alfajores* are shortbread-like biscuits from Argentina.
4 *Bobotie* is something like a curry with meat and dried fruit, and it has an egg topping. It's a South African dish.

File 36

Unit 7 Exercise 2

Simple ways to stand and move more at work

1 Take phone calls standing up. This also makes you sound more confident.
2 Use the stairs instead of the lift.
3 Walk to a colleague's desk, instead of sending an email or making a phone call.
4 Stand up and take a break from your computer every 30 minutes.
5 Don't eat your lunch at your desk. Go for a walk in your lunch break.
6 Stand during presentations or speeches.
7 Keep moving around. Take frequent breaks.
8 Ask your boss for a sit-stand desk.

File 39

Unit 7 Exercise 9

Role-play 1

Partner A	Partner B
You want to discuss a possible pay rise with your boss. Ask for an appointment.	One of your employees wants to talk to you but you have very little time as there's a crisis at the factory.

Role-play 2

Partner A	Partner B
You and your colleague both work shifts. Your colleague wants to speak to you about something.	You and your colleague work shifts. You want to ask if he/she will swap shifts with you next weekend.

File 45

Unit 8 Exercise 15

You are at an international conference and are having lunch with three other participants. You are talking about a presentation you all attended. Read about your communication style and think for a few minutes about what you are going to say. Make up any details you like, but stick to your role.

- You are not very talkative and would prefer to think about the presentation a bit more before you give your opinion.
- You would like to know more about the speaker's project results. From what she said, it's impossible to know if her results are really useful.
- You were not very impressed and will say so directly if someone asks you, but you always stay very calm and speak slowly and quietly.
- You don't use many gestures when you speak.

APPENDIX

Transcripts

Unit 1

Exercise 2, Track 2

There are special networking events at most trade fairs, and I have made some very good contacts that way, but you must prepare well. Find out who else will be there, and know what your goals are.

For me, more informal networking is very successful, too. Let me give you some examples. I spoke to someone at the booth next to ours who has shoe factories in Italy. Well, he gave me the right contacts to buy just the machines and leathers I was looking for. During lunch in the cafeteria one day, I found a distributor for Singapore. Then I found another one for Hong Kong over coffee at the coffee point near our booth. I found them both on the same day! We discussed the basics, and then they came over to Portugal to finalize the contracts.

I don't smoke, but the outside smokers' zone is an excellent place to make contacts. People are relaxed and so it's easy to start a conversation. That's where I met someone who actually became our US sales representative!

I always try to make the most of all the opportunities which come my way.

Exercise 11, Track 3

In my experience, staff in companies which operate internationally always use English names. It's not a personal preference but seems to be some sort of company rule. When I started working in an international firm, my boss asked for my English name on the first day and then always called me by that name. Many people find Chinese names difficult to pronounce, spell and remember, so when working with foreigners, we tend to use English names for convenience. It makes communication via email, phone or video with our US counterparts, for example, much easier. In my opinion, this is definitely the most important reason why we use western names in China.

I read somewhere that using a western name also shows a kind of respect to western culture. That is also the reason, at least according to what I have heard, why some foreigners who work in China give themselves Chinese names. Many people say that a new name means a new beginning! A friend told me that she sees this as a new trend in China. For example, more than half of the foreigners in her office have Chinese names. It is a positive way to get close to both work and life in China.

My first English name was Mary. My English teacher gave it to me because my family name is Ma. People often choose names which sound similar to their Chinese names. It also seems that many people prefer names which are easy to pronounce – like Emma or Anna. I thought Mary was a very common name, so I decided to change my name to Kelsi. I came across the name in a film called High School Movie! Some of my friends have the names of famous basketball players.

The meaning of a name is very important for many people so, for example, my friend Helen chose her name because it means shining light. When Chinese parents choose a name for their child, they always pay a lot of attention to the meaning.

One thing which can be confusing is the order of names. In China, we put the family name first. I think a lot of foreigners already know this, but even then when Chinese people do business internationally, they sometimes change the order and put their family name in second place!

Exercise 18, Track 4

Filipe: Hi. Welcome to our booth, I'm Filipe. I see you're looking at our vintage collection. May I ask your opinion on something?
Aoife: Er ... yes, certainly. Go ahead.
Filipe: Where do you come from, by the way?
Aoife: From Northern Ireland – from Belfast, actually.

Filipe: Well, I'd like to ask you something. What image do shoes made in Portugal have in Northern Ireland? We're in Milan at the moment, and everyone knows that Italian footwear has a great reputation for quality and style.

Aoife: Actually, you know the image of shoes from Portugal is just what attracted me to your booth.

Filipe: Really?

Aoife: Yes, I mean everyone knows that Italy has an excellent reputation for shoe manufacturing, but Portugal also has a long tradition of manufacturing good quality footwear, doesn't it?

Filipe: Yes, you're quite right. The Portuguese footwear industry has a long history of using the best quality materials and has the highest standards of workmanship. Take my company as an example, our shoes are made by hand, made of the finest leathers and have a very stylish design which has helped us create a strong brand. These are features people associate with Italian shoes, but we can compete with our Italian competitors on quality – and offer lower prices.

Aoife: Hm.

Filipe: May I ask you something about your company and what your particular interest is today?

Aoife: Let me introduce myself first. My name is Aoife Butler and I'm chief buyer for a chain of shoe shops in Northern Ireland. Here's my card. Our customers are young consumers who are both fashion and price-conscious, so we sell the latest styles at budget prices. My job now is to find suppliers for a second chain of more upmarket stores. We want to keep our image of selling cutting-edge fashion, but with better quality workmanship and higher quality materials – at higher prices, too, of course.

Filipe: I think we have a few collections which may interest you. Another thing you should know is that we have a reputation for being a socially responsible company – we're family-owned, we pay good wages and treat our staff very well. In the fashion industry today, this counts for a lot. But let me show you [...] So that's all I can show you today. I'd like to invite you to visit us in Felgueiras so that you see the full picture.

Aoife: Well, I must say, I'm very impressed with the collections you've shown me. I think that they're just what we're looking for. After you've sent over some samples for me to show my colleagues, we can talk about visiting the factory in F... how do you pronounce it?

Filipe: Felgueiras. Fel – guei – ras. Sounds like a good idea. I'll do that as soon as I get back. Well, if you'll excuse me, I have an appointment with a client from Singapore in a few minutes. It's been a pleasure meeting you A... oh, now I need some help with your name.

Aoife: It's Aoife. Aoife Butler. I'll look forward to seeing you again in Felgueiras.

Exercise 20, Track 5

Although trade shows are a great chance to display your products and meet people, it's not easy to stand out from the crowd of other exhibitors. It's all about getting potential customers to come to your booth and then making a strong impression on them. The way to do this is to have a digital presence before, during and after the show.

Use your social networks to create an event a few weeks before the trade show and invite all your fans to attend and share the link with their own contacts. Post information about special offers and competitions, and tell attendees exactly where to find your booth. Another good idea is to introduce the booth team with name, function and photo. You could also run a competition for attendees with prizes which can be picked up at the booth.

Then, on the first morning of the show, tweet a code word to all your followers. Anyone who comes to the booth and knows the code word gets a free gift or a discount on orders. Don't forget to post regular short updates on demonstrations, talks or receptions at the booth. Take photos during the show and post them. Interact with your followers during the show. Do all this and your company will stand out.

After the show, however, the work continues. It's very important to keep in contact with ...

Exercise 25, Track 6

1 Take that chewing gum out of your mouth.
2 Walk through hall six and turn left at the registration desk.
3 Come and join us for a glass of wine.
4 Make sure the appliance is disconnected, then open the back with a screwdriver.
5 Always send a follow-up email after the show.

Unit 2

Exercise 1, Track 7

A customer is someone who buys goods or services from a shop or a business. A manufacturer can be the customer of someone who provides raw materials.

We use the term client for someone who buys goods, or even more often services, which need personalization or customization. A client usually has a closer relationship with a company than a customer.

When we talk about consumers, we mean end-users. Consumers buy goods and services for their personal use.

Exercise 9, Track 8

Renata: Sonnentor Gmbh, Renata am Apparat. Wie kann ich Ihnen helfen?
Cleopa: Oh, I'm sorry I can't speak German. This is Cleopa Ayo from Tanzania. I'm the project coordinator of Muheza.
Renata: That's fine, Mr Ayo. Who would you like to speak to?
Cleopa: I'd like to speak to Gertrude Biedermann, please. I sent her an email to say that I'd call her.
Renata: Hold on a moment, please. I'll put you through.
Gertrude: Hello Mr Ayo, this is Gertrude Biedermann. It's nice to hear from you. Are you calling from Tanzania?
Cleopa: Hello Mrs Biedermann. I'm glad to talk to you too. I arrived in Germany yesterday.
Gertrude: I hope you had a good trip.
Cleopa: Yes, thanks. Everything went very smoothly. As I mentioned in my email, I'm going to be at the organic food trade fair in Nuremberg next week. I am phoning to see if we can arrange to meet there because I'd like to tell you something about our project. Would that be convenient for you?
Gertrude: That sounds like an excellent idea. I'll be at the fair every day. Just let me just check my schedule. Hm, shall we say late Tuesday afternoon or, let me see, early afternoon on Wednesday? Would either of those days suit you?
Cleopa: I'm available on both days, but Tuesday would suit me better. So I shall come to the Sonnentor booth some time on Tuesday afternoon?
Gertrude: Why don't you come at 4 pm? You'll have a good chance to see our products and probably meet some of our customers at the booth too. We are in Hall 7.
Cleopa: That sounds perfect. Thank you very much.
Gertrude: I'm looking forward to hearing about your projects.

Exercise 12A, Track 9

Our co-operative was founded two years ago to help the local farmers process the spices they grow. Our next step is to find markets for their products because we have to finance ourselves now. All our spices are grown according to strict organic standards, so that's why I got into contact with Sonnentor. You were recommended to me by our Dutch project leader.

Our main products are black pepper, lemon grass, cardamom and cloves. The conditions for growing these crops are just right. For example, we can harvest lemon grass for ten months per year. We also have modern machinery at our central factory, so the crops can be processed professionally.

Exercise 12B, Track 10

Cleopa: In Usambara, we drink tea with lemon grass for breakfast.
Gertrude: Really? That sounds refreshing!
Cleopa: I think there are many ways we could co-operate, so I'd like to invite Mr Gutmann to come to Tanzania to meet our farmers and see how we work. December or January are the best times. Could he make that, do you think?
Gertrude: Sorry, but I don't think he's free in December. There are a lot of events at Sonnentor before Christmas, but January is better. That sounds fine to me.
Cleopa: I am planning to visit our farmers in the Usambara mountains at the beginning of the year anyway, so how about middle of January?
Gertrude: Mr Gutmann is coming to the booth in about half an hour so we can check with him, but I'm sure that will be OK for him.

Cleopa: I'm sure he'll be very impressed with our products!
Gertrude: Do tell me some more about the way you ...

Exercise 19B, Track 11

1 I'd like to speak to Ms Martínez, please.
2 Philip isn't in the office today.
3 Oh hello, I didn't recognize your voice.
4 Is this a good time to talk?
5 She's in a meeting now. I think she'll be available after lunch.
6 I'm returning your call.

Exercise 19C, Track 12

1 **A** I'd like to speak to Ms Martínez, please.
B Please hold on. I'll put you through.

2 **B** Philip isn't in the office today.
A That's a pity. Could I leave a message for him, please?

3 **B** Oh hello, I didn't recognize your voice.
A Oh, I'm not surprised. I've got a terrible cold.

4 **A** Is this a good time to talk?
C Well, I have a meeting in a few minutes, but go ahead.

5 **B** She's in a meeting now. I think she'll be available after lunch.
A OK, then I'll try again later.

6 **C** I'm returning your call.
A That's great. I have a few things I'd like to discuss with you.

Unit 3

Exercise 5, Track 13

Amar

It depends on where my partners are because I work with clients on three different continents. A lot of the contact with my clients is face-to-face, so I have to check when people are taking their holidays. It's difficult to arrange a meeting with our French clients in August, for example, because everyone takes time off. Different holiday times can make it difficult to meet deadlines if the holiday period in one country is followed more or less directly by holidays somewhere else.

Different time zones can also make life difficult when we need to speak on the phone. I use a time converter app to check the time in different places. Actually, it's a time and date app because as there is no winter and summer time in India, it's easy to forget that the time may have changed in another country. I don't want my clients to wait an hour for my call!

Daniela

When I was working with a team based in Sydney, it was more or less impossible to arrange a web meeting at a time which was really convenient for all of us – especially in the winter. The only time possible was at 8 am our time, which was 6 pm in Sydney. So while we were not quite awake yet, the Sydney team was ready to go home! But it becomes even more difficult if you need to include people from three or four locations around the world. When we arranged a meeting at 8 am our time, our colleagues in Argentina had to be in the office at 4 am! We only did that once.

As long as we don't have to work 24/7 yet, I would say that the many different time zones are definitely the biggest problem!

Exercise 16, Track 14

Alessandro

When we decided to expand outside Italy, we were looking for a location with a good communication and transportation network. This is vital to guarantee an easy and efficient supply chain. Another important factor is the local labour market. We had to be sure that we could hire people with the skills needed to work at the plant.

In the case of Brazil, the production plant was a really good opportunity for us because the site was already an API production facility located in a major industrial area. The previous owners were a big multinational pharmaceutical company. This meant that when we bought the plant, the people, the basic working culture and the main operating procedures were all already in place, so we could start production very quickly.

Chen

At WiSMa we believe that the market for medical products and services in China has great potential. We need an office in the country in order to find partners in China.

For one thing, the Chinese economy is growing, so there's a big market for products and services from Europe. Chinese society is also getting older, so there is more interest in medical products. More and more people in China now have enough money to pay for medical treatment abroad. So we work with hospitals and clinics in Germany as well as Chinese travel agencies who specialize in this field.

Another reason for expanding to China is to help develop the exchange of expertise by organizing conferences in different fields of medicine. Hospitals in Germany and China show a lot of interest in developing these contacts.

Exercise 18, Track 15

Alessandro

When we took over the plant in Brazil, we signed an agreement to continue to employ the Brazilian workers who were already working there. At management level, we have a few European expats, but most staff are Brazilians who were hired after we took over. In the beginning, managers from Italy went over to supervise the operations, but now that's no longer necessary because everything is running very smoothly. We have regular conference calls, and everyone is comfortable using English as our working language.

There are many reasons why having local management is the better option for us. Let me give you one example. With expats in top positions, there's always a risk that people will only want to stay for 2 to 3 years and then return to Italy. This would involve too many costs and changes in managerial style.

Chen

For our kind of business, it would be impossible to build up a network of partners and distributors in China without Chinese staff who speak the language and understand the local business culture. The company, however, also needs staff here in Beijing who understand the way German, and European businesses in general, work. In addition, there's the question of language for communication between our office and the head office in Germany and our European suppliers.

I think everyone knows that a lot of Chinese students study in Germany. It's WiSMa's policy to employ Chinese staff who have studied and preferably also worked in Germany. Apart from German, they also have to be able to speak English.

While a lot of contact between Freiburg and Beijing takes place on the phone, by email or through web meetings, I also visit Germany, and my boss comes here fairly regularly in order to attend trade fairs or take part in conferences.

Exercise 21, Track 16

Dr Allen: Hello, I'm Jane Allen.
Mr Chen: It's nice to meet you, Dr Allen. Welcome to Beijing. My name is Chen.
Dr Allen: It's very nice to meet you too, Mr Chen. Thank you for all the information you sent us.
Mr Chen: Did you have a good flight?
Dr Allen: Yes, thanks. Everything was fine, but I expect you're wondering why we're the last to come out. Cemal – Professor Özdemir – is still waiting for his luggage.
Mr Chen: That's OK, we have plenty of time.
Dr Allen: Oh here he comes – with his suitcase!
Prof. Özdemir: Hello, sorry to keep you waiting. Someone had taken my case off the carousel and just left it at the side.

Dr Allen: At least it didn't cause a terror alarm!

Prof. Özdemir: Yes, thank goodness for that.

Mr Chen: It's nice to see you again, Professor Özdemir. Welcome to Beijing. Shall we go to the car? Let me take your case, Dr Allen.

Dr Allen: Thanks.

Prof. Özdemir: It's great to be here again. Are we staying in the same hotel as last time?

Mr Chen: It's a different one this time. It's more convenient for the conference venue. You know what the traffic is like in Beijing! Dr Allen, is this your first visit to Beijing?

Dr Allen: Yes, it is. I'm really looking forward to seeing a bit of the city. I hope we'll have enough time for that.

Mr Chen: Don't worry, we will. I've made arrangements for this evening to go to one of the famous Peking duck restaurants in the centre of the city.

Dr Allen: That sounds like a very good idea.

Mr Chen: Here's the car. During the drive into the city, I'll tell you about the people you're going to meet at the conference. Let me ...

Exercise 24, Track 17

Alex: Hi Maria, I'd like to discuss how the project is getting on. Time is short, so we need a clear picture of where we are.

Maria: Well, let me show you the present status. Look here, you can see that the software developers have completed their work as scheduled. They really worked around the clock to make that happen. So that means we can start the testing right away.

Alex: That's great news. I was afraid that we would have to delay testing until the beginning of next month.

Maria: No, that's not necessary. In fact, we're ready to start any time. I suggest that we get started ahead of schedule just in case there are any problems. That will give us a bit of breathing space. What do you say?

Alex: Yes, let's do that. Your team has done a great job, Maria. I'm very confident now that we can meet the deadline.

Unit 4

Exercise 7, Track 18

1 Well, jumping after Wirkola means that you are under lot of pressure to perform well. The person who did the job before you was very good. Bjørn Wirkola was the best ski jumper in Norway for several years in the 60s, so to jump after Wirkola was very difficult.

2 Doing something so the English can see it means to do something for show, to keep someone happy and without taking it seriously. The expression comes from Brazil and goes back to the 19th century. There was an international law to end slavery at that time. The British demanded that the Brazilians patrol their coast to make sure that boats didn't bring more slaves into the country. The Brazilian government, however, wanted to keep the slave trade going and so patrolled only for show for the English.

Exercise 11, Track 19

Dialogue 1

A There are a number of reasons why we are changing to this online project management software. One major benefit is that it offers inexpensive per-user licences. This means that we won't need a big investment for the software and infrastructure.

B I see what you mean. You definitely have a point there.

Dialogue 2

A Thank you for giving me the chance to talk to you again about the new equipment. Let me show you the results of our latest tests.

B That's very interesting, but you already know what I think. We're satisfied with the one we have, so I don't see the point in changing right now.

Exercise 15, Track 20

Volker: To begin with, / let me explain the parts / of our RC transmitter. //
Bart: What does RC stand for?
Volker: It means / radio control. //
Bart: Aha, of course. Oh, it looks very complicated to me!
Volker: Don't worry! // After our test flight, / you'll know / how it works. // These here / – you see – / are the control sticks. // You have to remember / that we're controlling / a three-dimensional flight. // The drone / can move from left to right, / backwards and forwards / and up and down. //
Bart: And the sticks control that?
Volker: Yes, / look, / it works like this. To the left, / to the right, / up, / down, / forwards / and backwards. // Shall I show you again? //
Bart: No, it's OK, I see.
Volker: Use your thumb / and index finger / to move the sticks. // It's easier / to get smooth movement / that way. // That's essential / to get a stable flight. //
Bart: Like this, you mean?
Volker: That's right. // Fine, / but rest your hands / on the transmitter like this. // They'll be more relaxed / in that position. // [...]
Volker: ... I think you've got the hang of it now. // Right, / so let's turn on the power again. // While the drone's flying, / you can see the position / on the display here. // I'll fly the drone to that position. // After that, / I'd like you / to move it down / to about two metres over the ground. // Do you think you can do that? //
Bart: I have to move the stick this way, right?
Volker: Yes, / that's right. // Great, / now finally, / bring it back / to where we started. //
Bart: Wow, I think I'm beginning to get the hang of it, but I can see that I still have a lot to learn. When's the next pilot training workshop?
Volker: There's one next week / in Austria, / but if that's too soon, / what about Valencia / in June? //
Bart: That sounds good.

Exercise 23, Track 21

Version 1

Good morning. We were asked to come up with some suggestions for improving our company website. We have been exploring other company websites and this helped us to develop a list of features that our site should have. This is our list. [...] Now we are looking for a web designer. Next week [...] The draft should be ready by the end of next month. Then the new website will be up and running by the middle of June.

Version 2

Good morning. It's nice to see you all. This morning, I'd like to give you an update on our plans to improve the company website. Debbie here and I have spent some time looking at other company websites, you know, to give us a bit of inspiration, and we've come up with a list of features that we think our site should have. You can see them on the slide. If anyone has any comments, please go ahead. [...] So, let's move to the next point. We're looking for a web designer. We'd welcome any suggestions from you, so please send me the names and contact details of anyone you'd like to suggest. We've planned to arrange interviews next week to [...] So that brings me to the end of our update. If everything goes according to plan, we hope to have a draft ready by the end of next month. If that works out, the new website should be up and running, on schedule, by the middle of June. I think that's good news, isn't it?

Unit 5

Exercise 4, Track 22

At our head office in London we only concentrate on our core activities. We outsource other business segments to external providers in different parts of the world.

We talk about offshoring when we work with a partner who is on the other side of the world. In our case this means in Bangalore in India. Our partners there provide IT support for our customers and database maintenance.

All the accounting work – like processing our payroll or invoicing our customers is done in Glasgow. I suppose that's an example of onshoring. That means working with a partner somewhere in the same country. This is the best solution when it's important to know the legal and tax regulations in the UK.

We've also started nearshoring some work to a partner in Poland. The colleagues there are part of our software testing team. Poland is not so far away – it's near, at least compared to India – and this can be an advantage when we need to arrange conference calls or web meetings.

Recently I heard the expression homeshoring and I suppose we do that too. Some staff from all departments work from their home offices a few days a week. Most people have certain tasks which they can deal with outside the office. They're all based in London, though, as they have to come into the office regularly. Homeshoring isn't outsourcing, it's another word for teleworking because the staff who do this are on our company payroll.

Exercise 8, Track 23

Camille: Thanks very much. I'm very impressed with the way you managed the rollout in Nigeria. It's very encouraging to get such positive results so early.

Amaka: Thanks, Camille. We're also very pleased over here in Abuja. I'm sorry I couldn't send the information earlier. I only received it myself the day before yesterday.

Camille: Don't worry, Amaka. We all have it now. Right, the next item on the agenda is schedules and deadlines. Not everyone's favourite topic, but we have a lot to do in a short time. So let's start with the ...

Amit: ... so it seems to me that we're making things very difficult for ourselves.

Camille: I see what you mean, Amit, but let me explain why the schedule is so tight. Our main competitor in India is going to launch their new version in August, so we need to be faster. In other words, we should finish this part of the project in a month's time. I know our original deadline was July, and I'm sorry, but we can't wait that long for the result. There is just too much time pressure from our marketing department.

Amit: Just to be clear, you mean our deadline is the middle of April? Uh ..., well, I think we can make it somehow, but I'll definitely need some extra staff if we ...

Camille: ... OK, Amit, so you go ahead as you suggest. So, let's ...

Amaka: Sorry to interrupt, but can I say something? The new schedule means that we need to collect more data on the online deals by, say, a week tomorrow, and send it over to the Mumbai team. Right?

Camille: Yes, but not only that, could you also think about the effects of the discounts you offered?

Amaka: Could you say please that again, Camille? The line is not very good ...

Exercise 13, Track 24

Speaker 1

Angélica mentioned that face-to-face meetings are the norm in Mexico. In Russia, too, it's important to invest time in getting to know the people you work with, but if we're talking about everyday communication at work, I think the communication channel people prefer is email. Of course, if it's a serious matter, people will meet – face-to-face or virtually, but, otherwise, I think they prefer to write an email or use instant messaging. If you want to speak to someone on the phone, it's a good idea to send an email first. If you just call, you will probably hear the answer: "Please write an email." So that's the opposite of what Angélica told us about Mexico. I suppose email is more flexible because you can deal with it in your own time, and people like to have things in writing.

Speaker 2

Angélica said that personal contacts are important in Mexico, and that's also true in India. India is another "spoken-word culture" where relationships make things happen, so if you want to get things done, it's definitely better to meet or at least make a phone call. When people meet, there is more opportunity to exchange information and clarify issues. The idea that using email saves time seems rather rude.

In fact, if you only ask for information or for action by email, this may also be interpreted as meaning it's not a very important issue. For example, if you're waiting for a delivery, it's a good idea to phone a few times to show that you need the goods as soon as possible. If you don't do that, the supplier won't think it's urgent.

Speaker 3

I come from Norway, but I think I can speak for other Scandinavian countries too. Angélica said that Mexicans like to communicate in person because, well, basically they like talking! I suppose that in Scandinavia we're a bit different. It's rude to take up other people's time if it is not really important. Generally, people prefer to communicate in writing because it's quicker, no one interrupts, and what you want to say is there in black and white. This is true for email and instant messaging. And if we use email, everyone can deal with it in their own time. No one would think it was rude to do that – so quite different from what Angélica said about Mexicans. Maybe we're more like the Canadians, but, for us, it's not only about "time is money".

Exercise 17, Track 25

1 So I'm arriving at 2 pm. Which hotel am I staying in?
2 The customer is very unhappy about the situation and wants to cancel the order.
3 There's a strike at the factory.
4 I'll be late.

Unit 6

Exercise 1, Track 26

Elano

I work in the petrochemical industry in Brazil. My company spent a lot of money on business travel in 2014, but spending fell by 10% in 2015. From what I know, this is about average for Brazilian companies.

Yang

The number of business trips in our company rises every year. The amount of money my company spent on business travel rose sharply in 2014 and increased slightly – by about 3% – in 2015. I think this is typical of many companies in China.

Haruto

In general, business travel spending in Japan has been low in recent years. This is also true for my company. In 2014, our spending was about 10% lower than the year before. It increased again by 8% the following year so maybe this is the start of an upward trend.

Darya

I work in the energy sector in Russia. In 2014 we reduced the number of business trips by 10%. That's quite a lot, but our spending rose sharply, in fact by 20%, in 2015. I think that's because of increased prices and not because the number of trips increased.

Scott

Business travel spending has remained about the same in my company since the financial crisis. I think this is also true for many other companies in the US. Our spending fell slightly – by about 2% in 2015, but I don't think is the start of a downward trend.

Exercise 3, Track 27

As a regional procurement manager at the European headquarters of a multi-national company, I'm responsible for most of Africa and the Middle East. I have a lot of contact with our suppliers in those areas. Personal contact is important, so I visit their factories and also attend trade fairs in the region. It's also a good way to find new partners and source new products.

My company has reduced the general travel budget by about 20% since I joined the company, and many colleagues tell me that the number of virtual meetings they take part in has risen by about 50%. For me, the cut in travel spending doesn't mean fewer trips, it simply means my visits are shorter now and that I have to bring back results!

Exercise 4, Track 28

I'm aware that many companies have reduced their travel budgets in recent years and have increased their use of virtual technology to replace face-to-face contacts. I've spoken to many business executives about this issue and, if you ask me, this is a mistake. Tele and video-conferencing technology has become easier to use and more reliable, but it can't provide the same chance to build strong relationships as a personal meeting. What's more, managers in companies which have increased their spending on business travel tell me that the decision-making process is quicker when people sit around a table together. I'd like to show you some figures to support [...] So, all things considered, paying for business travel is an investment and this shows your partners or clients that you think it's worth spending time and money to be with them.

Exercise 7, Track 29

1 Right, let's go to the reception desk first to get your security pass.
2 It's very nice to meet you at last. I hope you'll enjoy your visit.
3 That's our marketing department just down there.
4 So, that's the schedule for the next few days. Does that sound OK to you?
5 This is Ms Blanchard's office. She's expecting us at 10.
6 Do you live in the centre of Rotterdam or somewhere outside?

Exercise 10, Track 30

Scenario 1

Ole: Remember I told you about everyone in Norway's favourite cheese the last time I was here?
Janet: Er, yes, I think I do. There was something special about it, wasn't there?
Ole: That's right. Well, here it is. I've brought you some so that you can try it for yourself. Look, it's brown and it has a kind of caramel taste, it's slightly sweet, and it's something typically Norwegian.
Janet: Thank you, Ole. I love trying new kinds of food. I'll let you know how I like it.

Scenario 2

Ashton: By the way, here's a small gift from Mr Jenner. He told me he played golf with you the last time he was here, and asked me to give it to you.
Andreas: Thanks, Ashton. Yes, we did play, I remember. He's a very good player. Maybe this will bring me better luck when I play against him next time!
Ashton: Let's hope so. You can imagine why all our corporate gifts have something to do with golf!

Scenario 3

Jiang Jing: On behalf of my company, I'd like to present you with this very traditional gift. Please go ahead and open it.
Steven: Oh, thank you. It's beautiful.
Jiang Jing: It's very typical of Chinese culture. You know that dragons are very important in Chinese tradition. Dragons are a positive symbol, so we hope our business relations will develop positively.
Steven: That sounds good. I remember seeing a dragon dance the last time I was in China. Oh, you know we even have a dragon boat festival here every year now. They're very popular.

Exercise 12, Track 31

1
A Oh, that looks delicious. Is it a local specialty?
B Yes, in fact it's our national dish.

2
A Please have some more.
B Oh, I can't. I'm really full, thanks.

3
A So, shall I drive you back to the hotel?
B Well, it has been a very long day.

4
A Would you like another drink?
B That sounds like a good idea. But this one is on me.

5
A Maybe we can discuss this further over dinner.
B Well, I'm busy now, so how about tomorrow?

6
A Thanks for making us feel so welcome.
B It was a pleasure to have you here.

7
A Do you have children?
B Yes, two. Anyway, I think the taxi's waiting for us.

8
A So, we're meeting again at 9 am tomorrow. OK?
B Right, I have the schedule here.

Exercise 15, Track 32

1 Haggis is the most famous dish from Scotland. A dish similar to haggis was eaten something like a thousand years ago, so it's very traditional. It's a kind of pudding made of different parts of a sheep and cooked in the sheep's stomach. It doesn't sound or even look very nice, but it's very delicious.
2 This is Osechi. It's a traditional Japanese meal to celebrate the New Year. It includes many foods and each one has a meaning. The large prawn, for example, means long life because it looks similar to an old man who is enjoying life.
3 Well, this is a sort of soup made with coconut milk and a kind of cake made of sticky rice. It has pieces of jackfruit in it, which tastes a bit like chicken. Some people eat it for breakfast, but it can also be a main course at dinner. The name of the dish is lontong sayur. It's very popular in Indonesia.
4 It looks a bit like a piece of chicken, in a creamy sauce, but in fact it's a mild chili filled with meat and fruit. I suppose it's a kind of national dish in Mexico. The colours red, white and green are the colours of the Mexican flag, so people often eat on Independence Day. It's called chiles en nogada.

Exercise 20, Track 33

Conversation 1

A So what would you like to start with?
B Well, I'm not sure. Would you recommend this one here – number 14?
A I've never tasted it. Why don't you try it?

Conversation 2

A If you want to try a local dish, why don't you have the fish? It's delicious.
B Well, I'm a vegetarian so that's not really for me.
A Oh, I didn't know that. I'm sorry. Well, have a look at the next page. Those are the vegetarian dishes.

Conversation 3

A This is very tasty, I must say.
B I'm glad you're enjoying it. This is one of our favourite restaurants.
A Would you like another glass of wine?
B Oh yes, please. The wine's very good too.

Unit 7

Exercise 4, Track 34

On the one hand, companies can't always find employees with the skills they need with the result that they have to make the working environment more attractive. On the other hand, because of the high cost of real estate, companies have to use their office space more effectively.

So one way of combining these goals is to introduce activity-based working – a concept which comes from the Netherlands. The idea behind it is that the design of the workspace should support the different types of work which go on in a company, making it easier for staff to achieve their goals and increase their productivity.

Let me give you an example, many offices are designed for two activities – sitting at a desk or sitting in a meeting. This leads to a lack of flexibility. In an activity-based workplace, employees have the freedom to choose the most suitable location for each activity. They can go to a quiet area if they need to work in a concentrated way or they can collaborate with colleagues in an open space. Statistics from companies which have changed to activity-based working show that this has a positive impact on the innovation process in the company. People are just more creative when the environment makes it easier to talk and discuss new ideas.

Providing this flexibility does mean that employees give up their own fixed workstation, but they get the whole office in exchange. They can decide themselves whether they work in the office or at another location. This freedom of choice results in better job satisfaction – and a more effective use of office space.

In order to redesign the workspace to make the working processes more effective and efficient, it's my job to find out as much as I can about the tasks the staff do, what spaces they need to do them, how many people are in the office at one time, how many people come together at one time for meetings or informal talks – things like that. It's often surprising how little time employees actually spend at their desks or even in the office so, in fact, they don't need so much space. Reducing the size of the office enables companies to save costs, for example on rent and energy. My experience is that the change to activity-based working brings many advantages but, as I'm sure you can imagine, this means a big culture change for the whole company.

Exercise 8, Track 35

1 Unexpectedly, I'm going to be in Jakarta next week for a meeting, so I was wondering if we could move our appointment forward to next Tuesday. Would that suit you?
2 Good morning, Ms Hogan. It's Vitaly Antonov here. Can you give us the rollout date of the system modifications, please? We need this information as quickly as possible.
3 So you're saying that you would like to integrate the existing HR management system with the new IDM solution?
4 Good morning, Mr Oliveira. It's a pleasure to see you again.
5 Remember I told you about the problem at ATC? Do you have any idea how I can solve it?

Exercise 10, Track 36

Call 1

Nicola: Good, I'm glad we could solve that problem. It would be nice to have lunch together sometime to talk about more pleasant things.
Tetsuya: Yes, it would. Let's try to a find a date.
Nicola: Yes, let's do that. I'll be less busy after the meeting on Friday.

Call 2

Jan Breuer: Good morning, Mr De Vries. It's Jan Breuer speaking.
Bart De Vries: Good morning. What can I do for you?
Jan: I'm calling about our appointment on Monday.
Bart: Yes. Is there a problem?
Jan: Well, I have to leave for Milan on Monday afternoon, so I was hoping we could meet a bit earlier so that I can catch my plane.
Bart: We shouldn't call off the meeting, so let me see when I'm available. How about 11? Does that give you enough time to get to the airport?
Jan: Yes, that sounds good. That will give me plenty of time to ...

Call 3

Benedict: It's been very interesting talking to you, Jennifer.
Jennifer: Mmm. I can see a lot of potential for more co-operation. I was wondering if we could take the discussion further over lunch. Do you have time?
Benedict: I'd like to discuss the possibilities with you but, unfortunately, I have an appointment in a few minutes. Are you free this evening?
Jennifer: I'm driving home straight after the last talk today. I have to be back in the office tomorrow morning, you see.
Benedict: That's a pity, but we can get together another time.

Call 4

Elena: Hi Carlo. It's Elena here.
Carlo: Hi, how are you?
Elena: I'm good, thanks. Listen, Carlo, I was wondering if we could discuss the campaign. I know you're very busy, but it would be ...
Carlo: That sounds like a great idea. Would you prefer to have a web meeting or shall we get together here?
Elena: I'd prefer to meet. Would one day next week be possible for you?
Carlo: Let me see ... I have a lot of work to do next week, but I think I can make it on Tuesday.
Elena: Umm, that should be OK for me. Let me check a few things and I'll get back to you this afternoon. Is that OK?
Carlo: Yes, sure. Give me a call later.

Exercise 12, Track 37

1

Claudia: Right. So let's discuss the survey results. This is Ben, who carried out the survey, and he's going to take us through the main points. Rosa will bring up the points we've discussed among ourselves.
Ben: Thank you. Now, you've all had a chance to look at the results, so I'll be interested to hear your feedback, but let me start by explaining how this way of working will increase collaboration and productivity.
Rosa: Ben, may I interrupt you for a moment? I see your point, but I think the changes are going to have a negative effect on motivation.
Ben: I understand why you think so, Rosa, so let's take another look at the survey results.

2

Claudia: It would be very interesting to see the figures from other companies in the same business. Could you give us some information on that, Ben?
Ben: Well, I understand that the information would interest you, but I'm afraid it's against company policy to discuss other clients.

3

Claudia: Well, I think we've covered a lot of points this afternoon so that the impact of making these changes is quite clear now.
Rosa: I think you're right, Claudia. I feel much more positive about the idea now. Would you like me to organize a meeting with all the staff so that we can get everyone's opinion?
Claudia: That sounds like a very good idea. Please go ahead.

Exercise 16, Track 38

1 It's time to hear some facts and figures about the company.
2 And now we have more than 300 jobs all over the world.
3 We think it is very rude to give your opinion directly.
4 I hope to see you this afternoon.

Exercise 18, Track 39

Filipe

Attending trade fairs is one of the most important parts of my job as a business development manager, and I enjoy it a lot. The hardest part of my job is before the fair when I contact clients to invite them to visit us. What I enjoy most is when I see them at our booth! At a fair, I have the chance to explain the main features of our products and give information on our production capacity to buyers from all over the world. That's one of the best things about an international fair – both for me and for the company. We get into contact with so many people in a relatively short time. In the footwear industry, personal contacts are very important, and visitors can have a very positive effect on each other. For example, one of our clients wasn't happy with our latest collection, but when their buyer came to our booth and saw how many people were there – trying on shoes, asking questions, ordering – he realized that our products have a lot of potential. This resulted in more orders.

I suppose what I enjoy least are the times when there are not many visitors. Then I have to stand around with nothing much to do. Fortunately, this doesn't happen very often. However, to a certain extent this can also be positive because it gives me time to talk to people on the next stand and see what our competitors are doing. I've made some very good contacts that way. Exhibiting at trade fairs around the world is very expensive for companies, of course, in terms of money and time, but I know that everyone does their best to make the most of the opportunities of a trade fair.

Manish

Yoga is one of the most popular activities worldwide. People everywhere are doing yoga these days. What I enjoy most about my job as a yoga teacher and owner of a number of yoga centres is meeting and working with people.

Part of my work is to teach yoga classes free of cost at homes for senior citizens. All the senior citizens look forward to our weekly yoga class. In fact, one of my most amazing birthday celebrations was at a centre I worked at in Singapore, where the senior citizens baked a cake for me and arranged a little party! Even though my family was not with me in Singapore, I had found a family there.

Today, most people's jobs are all about a digital experience, but teaching is a people-centred profession. One of the best things about it is that I have the opportunity to teach people from different parts of the world. While I teach them yoga, I have the chance to learn about their cultures.

The hardest part of my job is that it can be physically exhausting because I'm teaching about five classes every day, so I suppose what I enjoy least is being very tired at the end of the day. However, I feel such a great sense of satisfaction when I realize that I've taught so many people that day. One of the most important parts of my job as a yoga teacher is that the classes help people on so many levels – they are fitter, more relaxed and have a positive influence on their families and colleagues.

Exercise 23, Track 40

I'm a technical manager for green building systems, so developing standards is one of the most important parts of my job. The hardest part of my job is to identify potential technical problems when building with wood and to develop strategies to solve them. What I enjoy most is when I see that my work encourages more people to use our green building solutions. The Chinese government has now recognized that wooden buildings are a good way of dealing with the challenges of environmental protection and support the development of green building solutions. Sometimes I'm frustrated if local committees don't accept our opinions, but I know that it may take more time for the local market to understand and accept the new system.

Fifteen years ago, there were no building standards for modern wood structures in China, but now many beautiful wood structures have been built in different regions in China. I'm quite convinced that wood is a really positive and sustainable solution for a green building strategy.

Unit 8

Exercise 7, Track 41

There are three different types of employees in my company: expats who are hired by the parent company abroad, local staff and, in my department, expats who are already living in Nigeria or other African countries. The contracts for each group can be very different in terms of salary and conditions.

So let me tell you what happens in my department if we want to recruit. The main channels we use are online applications, employee referrals and the services of recruitment agencies – in that order. We publish job vacancies on our website, and there's an online application tool that people can use.

In many cases, however, if there's a vacancy in a particular section, the Project Manager or Head of Department asks his staff for suggestions. Then he asks them to submit CVs of people they would like to recommend. In fact, that's how I got this job. It was through the recommendation of a friend who was working here at the time.

If the Project Manager has no candidate, he passes on the job description to our department and we do the recruitment. In that case, the first thing we do is to post the job vacancy on our website.

There are online job boards and job adverts in the newspapers that applicants make use of. They're quite popular with job-seekers, but I think getting a job through adverts like this is difficult because there are sometimes hundreds of applicants for every vacancy.

There are times when I believe "connections" matter a lot to land a job in big companies and small businesses. But I've also met a number of people working in big multi-national organizations who have found a job by replying to adverts they saw in the newspapers. And they had no connections at all. So it's not impossible!

One aspect I haven't mentioned so far is internal recruitment. This happens a lot when one project finishes and another begins. People often apply for jobs in the next project. Internal recruitment has lots of advantages, so if we get applications from our staff, we look at them very closely.

Exercise 10, Track 42

Sabine Meyer: Come in.
Morten: Good morning Ms Meyer.
Sabine: Good morning. Have a seat. How was your trip? You went home for a few days, didn't you?
Morten: Yes. I had a great time, thanks. It was our Constitution Day on Sunday. That's a very big celebration in Norway, you know, with huge parades and lots of ice cream and hot dogs! Everyone joins in and it's a lot of fun.
Sabine: Sounds nice. Anyway, I asked you to come so that we can discuss your work schedule for the second part of your internship.
Morten: Hm.
Sabine: But before we do that, let's take a look at how far you've got with the customer survey. I'm very impressed with the layout, and the questions are good. The idea to have some optional questions is a good one.
Morten: So far a lot of people have answered those questions, in fact.
Sabine: So how many responses have you received so far?
Morten: Let me check. So far we have a response rate of nearly 34%. That's about ...
Sabine: Excuse me for interrupting, can you remind me of the cut-off date for replies?
Morten: We still have two more weeks to go. What I wanted to say is that 34% is about average, but we need to improve on that figure.
Sabine: 34% is not bad, but, yes, I think we do need to get more replies. Sometimes it's helpful to offer an incentive for people to complete the survey. I don't think that's the case, at the moment, is it?
Morten: No, but I'll keep that in mind when I plan the next version.
Sabine: Good. The only other tip I can give you is to have a word with Dirk if you need any help.
Morten: That makes sense. Thanks, I'll do that.
Sabine: Right, so let's discuss your new work schedule now. Based on my observations of your work so far, I think you're the ideal person to deal with ...

Exercise 12, Track 43

When we hire edutainers, we look for people who have excellent communication skills, a solid background in science and technology and the ability to teach different target groups. This means that applicants for this job have to have knowledge, qualifications and talent.

The edutainers are responsible for answering all our visitors' questions, so they have to know a lot about a wide range of scientific topics. As an increasing number of our visitors are not Czech, we prefer to hire edutainers with good foreign language skills, especially English.

As the job title suggests, the most important part of their job is educating in an entertaining way. They need a very hands-on approach. You only have to see some of our shows and laboratory workshops to understand what that means. It's an edutainer's job to create interest in the topics and show how much fun science can be. Their audiences might be children, teenagers or adults, so an edutainer has to be able to present scientific phenomena at three different levels. Edutainers are involved in developing and delivering programmes for school groups, so they need the ability to connect with young people.

We're lucky that Techmania works in close co-operation with the University of West Bohemia in Pilsen, so we recruit many of our edutainers from there. Jiří, for example, who you can see here during one of his shows, is studying to be a science teacher. He has all the qualities and skills we're looking for.

Exercise 16, Track 44

George: Hi, may I introduce myself? I'm George Kaminski, but please call me George.
Jack: Ah hello ... er... George. It's very nice to meet you. My name is Jack Lee. Please take my card.
George: OK, thanks. Here's mine. How are you enjoying [...]
[...] So then before I got my MBA, I worked for Symtec for a few years as a systems analyst.
Jack: That's a very successful company. We worked with them on a very big project a few years ago. The co-operation went very well.
George: Yes, it was a great experience working for them. I really learned a lot there so that motivated me to study for an MBA.
Jack: I'm sure that was a wise decision.
George: Absolutely. I did the right thing! I've never regretted it even if it meant giving up a good job at Symtec.
Jack: I see that now you work for McBride.
George: Yes, I wanted to move into consulting, and my present job is a perfect fit for my qualifications and working style. But I've been talking all the time, now it's your turn to tell me something about yourself. Your company has a pretty impressive record too.
Jack: Oh, there's not so much to tell. My team is working on ...

Exercise 26, Track 45

Let me tell you something about my internship. The project I'm working on is fairly complex and so my work is demanding. Before I started work, I spent a few weeks getting to know the project by reading a lot and taking part in an e-tutorial for new staff. In that way, I did the same preparation as any new employee.

My supervisor introduced me to everyone in the department on the first day, but there wasn't really an opportunity for us to get to know each other. My impression so far is that the relationships between the staff are very work-related anyway. People don't seem to talk about any other topics. That's different from what I experienced when I was working in Norway. However, my supervisor and I have conversations about a whole range of topics. Of course, a lot is work-related, but during the lunch break, she asks me how I'm enjoying life here and gives me some tips about things to see and do in the city and the region.

The company has business partners in the Nordic countries, so she has often asked me about business culture in Norway and Sweden. But apart from that, I think she's planning a holiday trip to the Arctic Circle next year!

Another thing I've noticed which is different from Norway is that the hierarchy is more visible here. Everyone's position in the hierarchy is very clear. When I started working, I was told who is responsible for what. That's useful because I know who makes the decisions! Another aspect of a visible hierarchy is that I always have to stand up and shake hands with the Head of the Department whenever he enters the office, whereas in

Norway I could just say "Hello Kristin" to the CEO when I saw her. When I started working here, I sometimes heard people using first names with each other and thought I could do the same. Now I know that this is not the case! I also noticed that first names are not used as a general rule, even if people have worked together for a long time. For me, coming from Norway, this makes the working atmosphere feel quite formal. Of course, this may be because this is a very big company so there's more distance between people. Friends of mine who work in small companies in Germany tell a different story.

One very positive aspect of my job is that I have a lot of responsibility – within a certain framework, of course, but my boss and my colleagues trust me to do my job properly so this gives me good opportunities to develop my career. I'm learning a lot.

Film 1

Exercise 2, Track 46

For a company which produces and sells organic teas and herbs, it is essential to guarantee the highest standards at all stages of the supply chain. At Sonnentor, quality means product excellence, fair relationships with suppliers, and transparency towards customers.

Film 3

Exercise 2, Track 47

Building a good business relationship starts with first impressions. At the first meeting, we immediately notice clothes, body language and ways of greeting. What makes a positive first impression may differ from culture to culture as expectations can vary a lot. Think about your own expectations while listening to four young people talking about appropriate behaviour in their home countries.

Film 4

Exercise 2, Track 48

I study economy and regional geography at University of West Bohemia in Pilsen. This course, Edutainer Junior, is beneficial to my studies as I can apply my knowledge gained at university here. I like this work because I like to be in contact with people. The job is interesting and fun, and I find the people I meet positive. After my graduation I would like to be an engineer.

Video exercises APPENDIX

Film 1 – From field to table: Sonnentor GmbH in Sprögnitz, Austria

UNIT 2, PAGE 18

Before you watch

1

A Sonnentor GmbH produces organic teas, herbs and spices. The title of the film is *From field to table*. What do you expect to see?

B Which step in the journey from field to table does each photo below show? Use the quotes from the film to help you discuss. Do the photos and quotes match your expectations?

"Lots of our products are mixes which are mixed in our mixing drums."
"Apart from organic certification, we do testing here in our central factory."
"All the orders are packed with care by hand."
"This is our paradise for tea lovers."
"We sell the products in our own Sonnentor shops."
"We export to more than fifty countries."
"The mixes are sent to the packaging department."
"It's one of the first fully certified organic restaurants in Lower Austria."
"Let's find out what happens to the flowers and herbs after they have been harvested."

2

A 46 The narrator in the film is a native speaker of Mandarin Chinese. Listen to her and read along in order to get used to her accent. Underline any parts you find difficult to understand and replay the recording until you get used to the way she speaks.

"For a company which produces and sells organic teas and herbs, it is essential to guarantee the highest standards at all stages of the supply chain. At Sonnentor, quality means product excellence, fair relationships with suppliers, and transparency towards customers."

B Look at some typical features of a Chinese English accent. Do you notice any of them in the narrator's pronunciation?

China

Some features of pronunciation:
- with > [wit] or [wid]
- rice > [lice]
- first > [firs] (leaving out the final consonant of a word)
- equal stress on all syllables and words in a sentence
- emphasis on the last word of a sentence

While you watch

3

Watch the film and match the topics to the speakers.

	Johannes	Sonja	Josef	Manuela
1 exports	☐	☐	☐	☐
2 the product range	☐	☐	☐	☐
3 packing and labelling the products	☐	☐	☐	☐
4 the ingredients used in the restaurant	☐	☐	☐	☐
5 the history of the company	☐	☐	☐	☐
6 where the suppliers come from	☐	☐	☐	☐
7 the best-selling products	☐	☐	☐	☐
8 the future plans of Sonnentor	☐	☐	☐	☐
9 the production process	☐	☐	☐	☐
10 quality control	☐	☐	☐	☐
11 distribution channels	☐	☐	☐	☐
12 the range of products sold in the restaurant	☐	☐	☐	☐

4

A Watch each sequence (as shown) and answer the questions.

1 (**00:38 – 01:11**) a Why did Johannes start working with the organic farmers? b He mentions one important result of their co-operation. What is it?	

2 (**01:28 – 02:10**) a What organic products does he mention? b Why do the suppliers want to work with Sonnentor?	
3 (**02:20 – 03:16**) Manuela describes the production process after the herbs have been harvested. Complete the list of steps she mentions.	The first step is that the herbs and flowers are dried at the farms. Then they ____________[1] to Sonnentor in Spögnitz to our warehouse and afterwards they ____________[2] in the shakers in our ____________[3]. At Sonnentor we have more than 700 products – lots of them are mixes, which ____________[4] in our mixing drums. Afterwards they are sent to our ____________[5] department. The labels ____________[6] are printed here in-house in more than twenty languages. Afterwards they ____________[7] onto the products by hand to create jobs here in the region. Then they ____________[8] for delivery.
4 (**03:42 – 04:36**) a What do we find out about the shop in Sprögnitz? b Where can customers buy Sonnentor products?	
5 (**06:10 – 07:15**) At the restaurant called *Leibspeis*, Josef and Sonja talk about the dishes and the kinds of tea which are available. a What does Josef use the Sonnentor herbs for in his kitchen? b What kinds of tea are available from Sonnentor?	
6 (**07:40 – 08:01**) Johannes says that he started his business with three things. One of them was his father's leather trousers, what were the other two?	

B What do these numbers mentioned in the film refer to? Note down what you remember, then watch the film to check your answers.

1988 • 3 • 300 • €400 000 • 700+ • 20+ • 2008 • 50+ • 24 • 60 • 80 • 8 million

5

All the Sonnentor employees we meet in the film are native speakers of Austrian German. Watch parts of the film again and notice how they pronounce the words in *italics*. Did you find these words easy to understand?

1 (**01:02 – 01:04**) We decided to create *jobs* here.
2 (**04:05 – 04:06**) In two *thousand* and eight we developed a franchise system.
3 (**06:48 – 06:52**) We *try* to be a little different than anyone else *around* here.

After you watch

6

A Sonnentor has put the tiny village of Sprögnitz on the map. Visitors of all ages can visit the factory, take part in seminars and festivals during the year, walk along the nature trail, go shopping in the factory store and enjoy a cup of tea or a meal in the café or the restaurant. Write a short text to encourage visitors to come to Sonnentor.

B What could your company offer visitors? Write a promotional text to welcome visitors to your own company. Use your imagination!

7

A The narrator mentions an English saying: *The proof of the pudding is in the eating.* What does it mean? Is there a similar saying in your own language?

B Can you think of any common sayings in your own language which are connected to food and eating? Choose one and explain its meaning in English.

Film 2 – Made in Germany: service-drone in Berlin, Germany

UNIT 4, PAGE 34

Before you watch

1

What do you know about drones? Are these statements true (T) or false (F)?

1 ☐ Drones are operated by automated computer systems.
2 ☐ The rules for flying drones are the same all over the world.
3 ☐ It's illegal to take photos of people with a camera drone without their permission.
4 ☐ UAV (unmanned aerial vehicle) is the correct name for a drone.

2

A Label the parts of a drone with the words below.

camera mount • flight computer • engine • propeller • arm

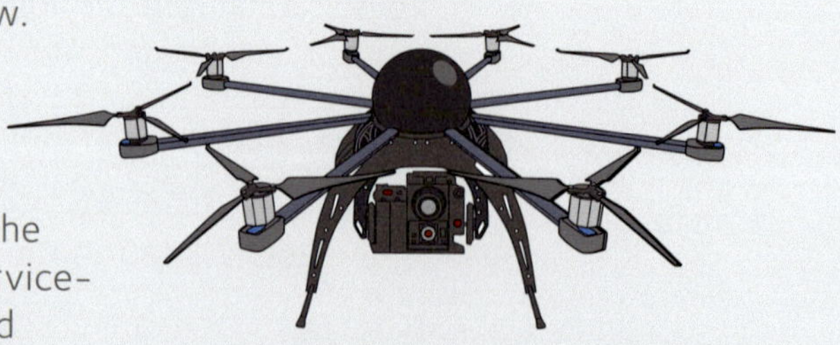

B At the beginning of the film Stephan Feldhoff, the international market development manager of service-drone, introduces the company. Use the words and expressions below to make up more sentences about the company. Add any details you like.

civilian-use drones • filming and movie production drones • go international • highly professional • manufacturer and developer • market leader • quality engineering

service-drone is …

We consider ourselves to be …

Because we see a need for …

While you watch

3 Listen to what Stephan says at the beginning of the film and compare what he says with the sentences you made up in **2B**. Were your predictions correct?

4 **A** Translate the words below. If the words have more than one meaning, choose the one closest to how you think it will be used in the film.

current	delivery	core
stable	reputation	screen
challenges	solar panel	aviation

B Watch the film and cross out the words in **4A** when you hear them for the first time. Tick the point in the film when you have crossed out the first complete row or column.

1 ☐ 05:28 2 ☐ 04:33 3 ☐ 02:54

C Watch the film until the end, and continue crossing out the words when you hear them. Which word didn't you cross out?

D Did you translate each word correctly? If not, correct your translations.

5 Watch each sequence (as shown) and answer the questions.

1 (**0:00 – 01:06**) What do we find out about service-drone from Stephan's introduction to the company?	
2 (**01:09 – 01:25**) What does the narrator tells us we are going to see in the film?	We are hearing more and more ______[1] about the huge ______[2] for drones. Let's find out from Stephan ______[3] and how the use of private and ______[4] drones can and will make ______[5].
3 (**01:25 – 01:43**) Civilian-use drones are used in many areas. Which of these does Stephan mention?	☐ crowd control • ☐ movie production • ☐ surveying • ☐ logistics • ☐ industrial documentation • ☐ repairs • ☐ mapping • ☐ agriculture • ☐ disaster management • ☐ nature conservation
4 (**01:43 – 02:16**) What seems to be the most important part of the drone? What reasons does Stephan give?	

5 (**02:18 – 02:57**) What is unique about the company?	
6 (**03:22 – 04:02**) a Which term or phrase in each pair does the narrator use? b Why is the camera mount we see so useful for film and TV productions?	a • **internal / innovative** activity • **cutting-edge / state-of-the-art** technology • **had to / hardly** vibrate during flight • to absorb the **flight / slightest** jerk or shake b ____________________ ____________________
7 (**04:55 – 05:38**) Stephan mentions two big challenges for the company in the internationalization process. What are they?	1 To identify, __________ [1], and __________ [2] a trustful __________ [3] with a number of foreign __________ [4]. 2 The __________ [5] regulation of each country is so __________ [6] that you actually need to apply different __________ [7] specifications to each and __________ [8] drone.

After you watch

6

A Create a short presentation about service-drone based on these photos.

B Look at your company's website and other promotional material and choose four pictures which show the most important aspects of your company's operations. Use them to give a short presentation of your company.

Film 3 – In my experience

UNIT 6, PAGE 48

Before you watch

1

A In the film, four young people talk about making a good first impression in their countries when travelling there on business. What advice would you give someone coming to your company for the first time? Think about the following topics.

1 dress code • **2** greetings • **3** communication style • **4** hospitality • **5** good/bad behaviour

B What do these pictures show? Which is the correct word or expression for each? You will hear all these terms in the film. Check any vocabulary which is new to you.

a banya ● **b** body language ● **c** business casual ● **d** clapping ● **e** curtsey ● **f** eye-contact ● **g** facial expression ● **h** flashy jewellery ● **i** interrupting ● **j** poker-faced ● **k** punctuality ● **l** traditional clothing

C Categorize the words and expressions in **1 B** according to the topics below.

1 dress code ____________ 4 hospitality ____________

2 greetings ____________ 5 good/bad behaviour ____________

3 communication style ____________

2

47 Listen to the audio recording of the introduction to the film and complete the text.

Building a good business ____________ [1] starts with first ____________ [2]. At the first meeting, we immediately notice clothes, body language and ways of ____________ [3]. What makes a positive first impression may differ from culture to ____________ [4] as expectations can vary a lot. Think about your own ____________ [5] while listening to four young people talking about appropriate ____________ [6] in their home countries.

While you watch

3

Watch the film and match the topics to the speakers.

	Aureen	Mohit	Sarfaraz	Valeria
1 dress code	☐	☐	☐	☐
2 eating out	☐	☐	☐	☐
3 eye-contact	☐	☐	☐	☐
4 ways of greeting	☐	☐	☐	☐
5 interrupting	☐	☐	☐	☐
6 punctuality	☐	☐	☐	☐
7 respect	☐	☐	☐	☐
8 importance of culture	☐	☐	☐	☐

4 Watch each sequence (as shown) and answer the questions.

1 (**01:06 – 01:26**) How can you expect to be greeted in Nigeria? a by a female business partner b by a male business partner c by a group of people	
2 (**01:50 – 02:27**) What will make a negative impression on your Nigerian business partners?	
3 (**02:33 – 02:30**) What can you expect from your hosts if you go to India on business?	
4 (**03:00 – 03:15**) Mohit says that Indians are good at multi-tasking. Which two examples does he give?	
5 (**03:30 – 04:23**) How does Mohit greet Aureen?	
6 (**04:26 – 05:25**) a What questions does Valeria ask Sarfaraz? b How does Sarfaraz confuse Valeria?	
7 (**05:25 – 06:12**) a How do people in Pakistan show respect? b Who is it very important to show respect to?	
8 (**06:12 – 07:06**) What did Sarfaraz experience when he started his diploma programme in New Zealand?	
9 (**07:14 – 08:18**) a Why are the clothes you wear so important in business in Russia? b Valeria gives some advice on a suitable dress code. Which are the two most important pieces of advice in your opinion?	
10 (**08:18 – 08:36**) How do Russian hosts show their hospitality?	

After you watch

5 **A** At the beginning of the film, Aureen says that people sometimes think about Africa as if it is a country, not a continent. What effect does this have?

B Valeria quotes a Russian proverb: “First you judge how nice, then you judge how wise.” What could the proverb mean? Consider what she talks about in the film.

C Mohit mentions Diwali. What does he say about it?

6

A Read about some features of English spoken in India, Nigeria, Pakistan and Russia. Did you notice any of these features when you watched the film? If so, did they cause any misunder-standings or did they make it easier to understand the speaker?

India

Some features of pronunciation:
- there > [dere] or [tere]
- water > [vater] vehicle > [wehicle] (no difference between w and v)
- tendency to give the same stress to all words in a sentence
- more frequent use of progressive verb forms

It is difficult to generalize because there are many differences in the pronunciation of English spoken in India depending on the region, native language, educational background, etc. of the speakers.

Nigeria

Some features of pronunciation:
- speaking > [speakin]
- there > [dere] or [tere]
- making uncountable words countable e.g. *informations* instead of *information*
- frequent use of *could* and *would* instead of *can* and *will*
- tendency to give the same stress to all words in a sentence and to each syllable of a word

There are big differences in the pronunciation of English spoken in Nigeria because of the large number of native languages.

Pakistan

Some features of pronunciation:
- hand > [and]
- water > [vater]
- vehicle > [wehicle] (no difference between w and v)
- tendency to give the same stress to all words in a sentence
- more frequent use of progressive verb forms

Russia

Some features of pronunciation:
- there > [dere] or [zere]
- water > [vater]
- vehicle > [wehicle]
- short and long vowels sound the same
- leaving out articles e.g. *I am engineer* instead of *I am an engineer*
- adding unnecessary articles e.g. *it's a good to …* instead of *it's good to …*

B Watch these sections of the film again. Listen carefully and fill in the missing words.

Aureen (**00:48 – 00:58**)	On entering the country, it is very ______ [1] to see people, both male and female, ______ [2] the traditional clothing, which is very colourful.
Mohit (**03:04 – 03:14**)	For example, if you're having a conversation with a ______ [1], suddenly some person would come and ______ [2] you in-between. And also it's very ______ [3] to talk over the the phone and talk to the other person on the same time. So we are good at multi-tasking ______ [4].
Sarfaraz (**05:26 – 05:35**)	In Pakistan, people ______ [1] making eye-contact with their ______ [2] even when they are discussing, either it is an important meeting or a day-to-day ______ [3] talk, they don't make eye-contact.
Valeria (**07:25 – 07:45**)	But if you want to be successful in your business meeting with your Russian ______ [1], you should be aware that clothes in Russia show your status. So, for men, it's ______ [2] to wear black ______ [3] with expensive shoes. For ladies, it's a good to wear skirt, knee-length, with ______ [4] shirt.

7 Considering what Aureen, Mohit, Sarfaraz and Valeria say about the norms in their countries, what advice would you give each one on how to make a good impression in your country/ company? Think back to your answers to exercise **1 A**.

It's the same here, it's a good idea to ...

Here it would be a good idea to ...

It's not necessary to ...

Film 4 – Lighting the fire: Techmania Science Centre in Pilsen, Czech Republic

UNIT 8, PAGE 65

Before you watch

1 Read the comments about skills shortages in Canada, the UK and USA. Discuss how much of a problem this is in your area.

UK
Employers can't find candidates with the right skills for more than one in five job vacancies. Dealing with the skills shortage in STEM-related fields is an urgent matter.

USA
Many companies, from Silicon Valley start-ups to established multi-national giants, report serious problems filling STEM jobs.

Canada
Without an increasing number of students graduating in the STEM professions, the negative impact on the science and technological industries will affect the whole economy.

S = science T = technology
E = engineering M = mathematics

2 48 All the staff we meet at Techmania are native speakers of Czech. In order to get used to a Czech accent, listen to an audio recording of Alžběta before you watch *Lighting the fire* and complete the text.

I study Economy and ______[1] Geography at ______[2] of West Bohemia in Pilsen. This course, Edutainer Junior, is beneficial to my studies as I can ______[3] my knowledge gained at ______[4] here. I like this work because I ______[5] in contact with people. The job is ______[6] and fun, and I find the people I meet ______[7]. After my graduation I would like to be an ______[8].

While you watch

3 The film gives us the answers to questions 1 – 6 below. Watch the film to find out which speaker answers each question. Then note down the answers.

	Alžběta	Alena	Jiří	Miroslav
1 Who are Techmania's target customers?	☐	☐	☐	☐
2 What does an edutainer do?	☐	☐	☐	☐
3 How can visitors learn about the effects of liquid nitrogen?	☐	☐	☐	☐
4 What is a benefit of the Edutainer Junior programme?	☐	☐	☐	☐
5 How many visitors does Techmania hope to welcome this year?	☐	☐	☐	☐
6 What does Techmania do for science teachers?	☐	☐	☐	☐

4 Watch each sequence (as shown) and answer the questions.

1 (**00:00 – 00:41**) a What problem are companies facing today? b What is the role of science centres in helping solve the problem?	
2 (**00:41 – 01:38**) a Which two organizations established Techmania? b How does Techmania aim to introduce scientific knowledge to children and the general public?	
3 (**02:21 – 03:14**) a What are Jiří's career plans? b What does he do during the show about liquid nitrogen?	a ____________________ ____________________ b He can ____________ [1] rubber to ____________ [2] it with hammer. He can also make ____________ [3] explode.

4 (**03:51 – 04:19**) a Here we see two teachers preparing to bring their classes to Techmania. What is the topic of the exhibit they are looking at? b Which aspects of this topic do we see in the film?	
5 (**04:44 – 05:37**) Alena mentions the international focus of her work at Techmania. What examples does she give?	We are exhanging ______[1] with our partners. We are also part of Ecsite, the ______[2]. We work on a lot of European projects, for example on the RRI, the Responsible Research and ______[3], or on the EEED project, the European Exhibition Evaluation Tool which aims to prove that ______[4].
6 (**05:39 – 07:35**) Miroslav mentions the approach to learning which is promoted at Techmania (including the Engineer project). What are the principles of the programmes?	

After you watch

5

A Read about some features of English spoken by Czech native speakers. Did you notice any of these when you watched the film? If so, did they cause misunderstandings?

> **Czech Republic**
>
> Some features of pronunciation:
> - there > [dere] or [vere]
> - water > [vater]
> - wait > [waid]
> - tendency to pronounce words as they are written
> - tendency to give the same stress to all words in a sentence
> - leaving out articles
>   e.g. *I work for marketing department* instead of *I work for the marketing department.*

B Listen carefully to these sections of the film again and fill in the missing words.

1 (**03:06 – 03:09**) We can freeze rubber to break it ______.

2 (**03:24 – 03:29**) I study economy and ______ at ______ of West Bohemia in Pilsen.

3 (**04:44 – 04:52**) My name is Alena, and I'm ______ at Techmania for marketing department and for international projects.

6

A Read this list of topics from the film. Discuss with a partner what you remember about each one.

ŠKODA • formal and informal learning • edutainers • saving energy • travelling exhibitions • educational programmes

B Look at the pictures of some of the interactive exhibits in the edutorium at Techmania. Do you think science centres like Techmania can "light the fire" of interest in science and technology?

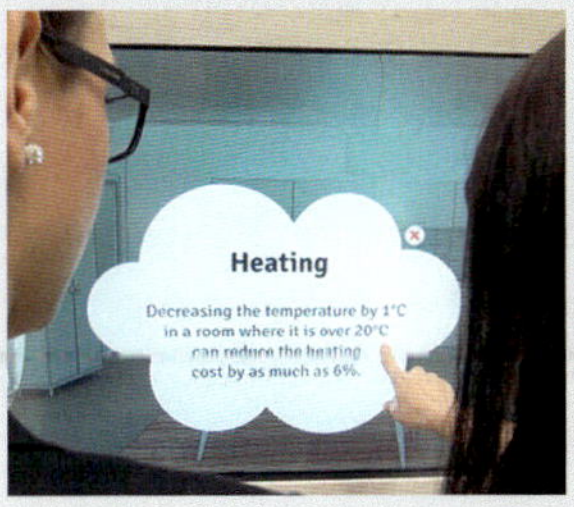

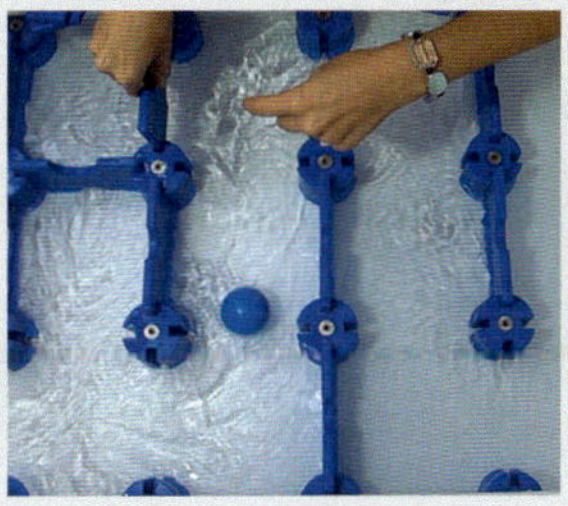

APPENDIX

Answer key – progress check

Exercises requiring personalized responses do not appear in the answer key.

Unit 1 page 13

24

1 E (Now, last but not least, I would like to introduce our marketing director.); **2** C (Our plan is to make the most of the trade fair next week.); **3** A (Although there were long queues at the conference he made the best of the situation by networking with possible clients.); **4** B (The worst case scenario would be that we receive no orders for our latest model.); **5** D (The best practice has proved to be a focus on company ethics.)

25

A **1** E (Go straight to the buyer and apologize for the mistake.); **2** B (Pass through the entrance to the conference hall and you will find our stand on the left.); **3** D (Join us for dinner this evening!); **4** C (Finish giving out the business cards, then make an appointment with Ruby Sandler.); **5** A (I suggest talking to David Grant.)

C Suggested answers
1 Why don't you come and join us for a glass of wine?; **2** First of all, make sure the appliance is disconnected, then open the back with a screwdriver.; **3** It's a good idea to always send a follow up email after the show.; **4** Please take that chewing gum out of your mouth.; **5** You can walk through hall six and turn left at the reception desk.

26

A Suggested answers
1 It's nice to finally meet you.; **2** May I introduce my colleague?; **3** Shall we exchange business cards?; **4** Excuse me, do you know the way to canteen?; **5** I'm very interested in the work of your research department.; **6** If you'll excuse me, I must go to the project kick-off meeting.; **7** Please don't forget to send me the information regarding the conference.; **8** I'm sorry but I have forgotten the price of your product.; **9** OK, thanks. I look forward to hearing from you.; **10** When I get back, I'll make sure to update you on any progress we have made.

Unit 2 page 21

18

1 provides, trades; **2** is supplied; **3** are authorized; **4** organizes; **5** is planned; **6** hope

19

A **1** line; **2** back; **3** put you through; **4** message; **5** Thanks

20

1 How soon can you deliver the first batch?; **2** How far is the nearest port?; **3** How many litres do you produce per year?; **4** How big is your workforce at this location?; **5** How long is the total transit time between Shanghai and Rome?; **6** How many different products do you stock?

Unit 3 page 29

23

A **1** G; **2** E; **3** H; **4** A; **5** F; **6** D; **7** B; **8** C

24

A **1** time is short; **2** as scheduled; **3** right away; **4** delay; **5** ahead of schedule; **6** meet the deadline

B *working around the clock* – working hard without stopping
to give someone breathing space – to take the pressure off someone

C **1** time off; **2** overtime; **3** time pressure; **4** in time
Suggested answers
At the moment we are working two days *behind schedule.*
Due the engineer's *busy schedule* she did not have time to come to the construction site.
Both the manager and his deputy took extended *time-out*.

25

A **1** merge; **2** sell; **3** assemble; **4** take over; **5** trade; **6** source; **7** recruit; **8** purchase

B Suggested answer
Research – to investigate a subject for business or scientific purposes

Unit 4 page 37

22

A **1** such; **2** among; **3** definitely; **4** all this; **5** work

B **1** market leader; **2** close relationship; **3** innovative technology; **4** environmental impact; **5** low-maintenance; **6** environmentally sustainable; **7** added advantage; **8** urgent need; **9** reasonable cost

23

B Suggested answers
Version 1 The speaker is more monotonous and overly formal.; **Version 2** The tone of the speaker is friendly and more conversational. This version is more effective because the speaker makes an effort to engage with their colleagues, helping them understand what has been done and asking for their advice.

24

Suggested answers
Situation 1 The best thing to do would be to make a personal visit to the company's offices.; **Situation 2** I'd suggest that you prepare some opening phrases in French.; **Situation 3** It would help if you asked all your contacts to inform you when they hear of any vacancies.

Unit 5 page 45

17

Suggested answers
1 She phoned to say that she's arriving at 2 pm and wanted to know which hotel she is staying at. / ... wanted to ask ...; **2** She phoned to say that the customer is very unhappy about the situation and wants to cancel the order.; **3** She phoned to say that there was a strike at the factory. / ... there is a strike ... ; **4** She phoned to say that she will be late. / ... she would be late.

18

1 wrong; **2** words; **3** after; **4** mean; **5** far

19

A Suggested answers
a Can we start with an update from everyone?; **b** Is everyone with me? **c** What's happened?; **d** What's your position on this, Fabio?; **e** John, I have a question for you.; **f** I'm very happy with the way you managed the rollout.

B **1** b; **2** d; **3** f; **4** a; **5** c; **6** e

Unit 6 page 53

20

A **Conversation 1**: b, j; **Conversation 2**: h, i, j; **Conversation 3**: k, e, a

B **1** b; **2** b; **3** a; **4** b; **5** a

Unit 7 page 61

21

1 see; **2** yesterday; **3** and; **4** everyone; **5** me; **6** meeting

22

1 a and c are ways of making arrangements. b is a way of asking for help.; **2** a and b are ways of asking to discuss something new. c is a way of politely disagreeing.; **3** a and b are ways of checking what someone has said. c is a way of asking someone to reformulate what they have said.; **4** b and c are ways of mentioning something at the end of a meeting. a is a way of reformulating what someone has said.

23

A **1** Helen is a technical manager for green building systems.; **2** The material she works with is wood.; **3** She talks about the success of encouraging more people to use her green building solutions and making the Chinese government recognize that wooden buildings are a good way of dealing with environmental challenges.; **4** She is frustrated when local committees don't accept the opinions of her team.

B Some features of Chinese English pronunciation are: with > [wit] or [wid]; rice > [lice]; first > [firs] (leaving out the final consonant of a word); equal stress on all syllables and words in a sentence; emphasis on the last word of a sentence

Unit 8 page 69

23

1 promotion; **2** vacancies; **3** position

24

1 Morten has to spend a few weeks reading a lot and taking part in an e-tutorial, like any new employee; **2** staff only talk about topics related to work; **3** they talk about a range of topics during the lunch breaks; **4** everyone's position and responsibilities are made very clear, Morten has to stand up and shake the Head of Department's hand, he is not always able to use first names with colleagues

Acknowledgements

Photos

Cover: Marco Baass, Berlin | **p. 2:** Shutterstock, chungking | **p. 3:** von links nach rechts: Angela Lloyd; Marchién Bel; Angela Lloyd; unten: Shutterstock, lculig | **p. 4:** von links nach rechts: Shutterstock, Matej Kastelic; Shutterstock, Marcin Balcerzak; Shutterstock, chungking; Shutterstock, auremar | **p. 5:** von links nach rechts: Rani Kumar; Quattro a/v group; Shutterstock, Rawpixel; Anna Batrla | **p. 6:** oben: von links nach rechts: Angela Lloyd; Marchién Bel; Angela Lloyd | **p. 9:** Angela Lloyd | **p. 11:** Sozé | **p. 12:** oben: Shutterstock, Matej Kastelic; unten: Shutterstock, Vichy Deal | **p. 13:** Shutterstock, Lars Zahner | **p. 14:** oben: von links nach rechts: Shutterstock, Marcin Balcerzak; Shutterstock, Firma V; Shutterstock, s_oleg; mitte: von links nach rechts: Shutterstock, SpeedyKingz; Sutterstock, Sergey Ryzhov; unten: von links nach rechts: Rani Kumar; Mohan Kumar | **p. 16:** Rani Kumar | **p. 17:** Quattro a/v group | **p. 18:** mitte: Sonnentor; unten: Quattro a/v group | **p. 19:** Mauritius images, Cultura | **p. 21:** Fotolia, auremar | **p. 22:** von links nach rechts: Shutterstock, A and N photography; Shutterstock, auremar; Shutterstock, Dmitry Kalinovsky | **p. 23:** Shutterstock, holbox | **p. 26:** links: Chemi; rechts: WisMa | **p. 27:** links: Chemi; rechts: Angela Lloyd | **p. 28:** Shutterstock, chungking | **p. 29:** Rani Kumar | **p. 30:** oben: von links nach rechts: Shutterstock, gallofoto; Fotolia, graf; Shutterstock, Madarakis; Shutterstock, Denys Prykhodov; Mitte von links nach rechts: Shutterstock, Oleksiy Mark; Shutterstock, StockPhotosArt | **p. 31:** von oben nach unten: Piacentini Costruzione SpA; WeDoTech; Quattro a/v group | **p. 32:** Shutterstock, PhotoStock10 | **p. 33:** Shutterstock, auremar | **p. 34:** beide: Quattro a/v group | **p. 36:** Shutterstock, Dynamicfoto (1–6) | **p. 37:** Shutterstock, l i g h t p o e t | **p. 39:** Shutterstock, Saibarakova Ilona | **p. 41:** Rani Kumar | **p. 43:** Anna Batrla | **p. 45:** Rani Kumar | **p. 47:** oben: Marchién Bel; unten: Shutterstock, Michal Kowalski | **p. 48:** Marchién Bel (1–6); unten: Quattro a/v group | **p. 50:** oben: Marchién Bel (1–3); unten: Shutterstock, Pressmaster | **p. 51:** von links nach rechts: Shutterstock, JPL Designs; Shutterstock, Norman Pogson; Angela Lloyd; Shutterstock, yasuhiro amano | **p. 52:** Shutterstock, Janis Lacis | **p. 53:** Shutterstock, Rido | **p. 54:** Active Working CIC | **p. 55:** Rani Kumar | **p. 56:** Valeria Federova | **p. 57:** Shutterstock, Brian A Jackson | **p. 58:** Shutterstock, Rawpixel | **p. 59:** Shutterstock, Iakov Filimonov | **p. 60:** links: Total Yoga; rechts: Sozé | **p. 61:** Angela Lloyd | **p. 63:** Shutterstock, Daniel M Ernst | **p. 64:** Anna Bartla | **p. 65:** beide: Quattro a/v group | **p. 67:** Shutterstock, Air Images | **p. 69:** Anna Bartla | **p. 72:** Shutterstock, aopasan | **p. 76:** Shutterstock, Bukhavets Mikahil / p.77: Shutterstock, aopsan | **p. 82:** Shutterstock, Dynamicfoto | **p. 83:** Shutterstock / Dynamicfoto | **p. 84:** WisMa | **p. 103:** oben: alle: Quattro a/v group; mitte: alle: Horst Preier; unten von links nach rechts: Horst Preier; Marchién Bel; Quattro a/v group | **p. 104:** oben: Angela Lloyd; mitte: Quattro a/v group (1–4) | **p. 106:** Horst Preier | **p. 108:** Quattro a/v group (1–4) | **p. 109:** oben: von links nach rechts: Shutterstock, Nikolay Dimitrov – ecobo; Shutterstock, okonart; Shutterstock, michaeljung; Shutterstock, baranq; mitte: Quattro a/v group; unten: Quattro a/v group (1–4) | **p. 112:** Quattro a/v group | **p. 113:** Quattro a/v group (1–3) | **p. 115:** Quattro a/v group (1–4)

Illustrations

p. 6, 7, 15, 27, 32, 40, 49, 54, 66, 106: Natascha Römer, RÖMER & OSADTSCHIJ – Visualiesierung GbR, Schwäbisch Gmünd

Track list

Track	Exercise	Length
01	Copyright	00:10
Unit 1		
02	Exercise 2	01:15
03	Exercise 11	02:51
04	Exercise 18	03:22
05	Exercise 20	01:32
06	Exercise 25	00:41
Unit 2		
07	Exercise 1	00:41
08	Exercise 9	02:07
09	Exercise 12A	00:58
10	Exercise 12B	00:57
11	Exercise 19B	00:43
12	Exercise 19C	00:59
Unit 3		
13	Exercise 5	01:56
14	Exercise 16	02:01
15	Exercise 18	02:14
16	Exercise 21	01:42
17	Exercise 24	00:59
Unit 4		
18	Exercise 7	00:57
19	Exercise 11	00:50
20	Exercise 15	02:05
21	Exercise 23	01:55
Unit 5		
22	Exercise 4	01:40
23	Exercise 8	01:57
24	Exercise 13	02:49
25	Exercise 17	00:34

Track	Exercise	Length
Unit 6		
26	Exercise 1	02:00
27	Exercise 3	00:52
28	Exercise 4	00:59
29	Exercise 7	00:48
30	Exercise 10	01:57
31	Exercise 12	01:38
32	Exercise 15	01:35
33	Exercise 20	01:08
Unit 7		
34	Exercise 4	02:31
35	Exercise 8	01:02
36	Exercise 10	02:19
37	Exercise 12	01:36
38	Exercise 16	00:34
39	Exercise 18	03:27
40	Exercise 23	01:22
Unit 8		
41	Exercise 7	02:44
42	Exercise 10	02:00
43	Exercise 12	01:48
44	Exercise 16	01:23
45	Exercise 26	02:29
Film 1		
46	Exercise 2	00:29
Film 3		
47	Exercise 2	00:35
Film 4		
48	Exercise 2	00:37

Clarity Studio Berlin
Direction: Christian Schmitz
Sound engineers: Christian Schmitz, Pascal Thinius
Speakers: Aureen Aipoh, Victor Bashkatov, Morten Berg, Aneta Cakarska, Marienne Graffam, César Holanda, Tetsuya Hori, Anna Knaifel, Manjul Kumar, Uta Kural, Ali Mazlooman, Jeffrey Mittleman, Albert Moshi, Merlene Perera, Laure Périsse, Christian Schmitz, Simon Srebrny, Frans van Tartwijk, Yuetiping Yu, Liang Zhipang